TIME
TRAVEL
FOR
BEGINNERS

TIME TRAVEL FOR BEGINNERS

MARY & JOHN GRIBBIN

Hodder Children's Books

A division of Hachette Children's Books

Text Copyright © 2008 John Gribbin and Mary Gribbin
Illustrations Copyright © 2008 Martin Aston

First published in Great Britain in 2008
by Hodder Children's Books

1

A Catalogue record for this book is available
from the British Library

ISBN 978 0 340 95702 8

Design and diagrams by Tony Fleetwood

Printed and bound by CPI Bookmarque Ltd, Croydon, Surrey

The paper and board used in this paperback by Hodder Children's Books are natural
recyclable products made from wood grown in sustainable forests. The manufacturing
processes conform to the environmental regulations of the country of origin.

Hodder Children's Books
a division of Hachette Children's Books
338 Euston Road
London NW1 3BH
An Hachette Livre UK Company
www.hachettelivre.co.uk

Acknowledgements

The idea for this book grew out of a discussion with Margaret Conroy, and became a reality thanks to the University of Sussex and its excellent library facilities, and the generosity of the Alfred C. Munger Foundation in contributing to our travel and other expenses. Many years ago, our interest in science fiction in general was stimulated by Harry Stead, and in time travel in particular by a conversation with Fred Hoyle. More recently, Igor Novikov convinced us that time travel might be fact, not fiction. Special thanks to Hugh Jeffery and to Jack Railton-Woodcock for reading the entire text and making us explain things more clearly.

Contents

Introduction

What Isn't Forbidden is Compulsory

Scientists have found the law of nature that permits time travel –
the same law that makes sure that light travels in straight lines.

The opening of the door of possibility for time travel involves the
two greatest ideas in twentieth-century physics: general
relativity and quantum mechanics. This book will explain the
elements of general relativity and quantum mechanics involved
in the theories of time travel – but don't be scared!

These big ideas used to be regarded as terrifyingly difficult, but that was only because they were new and different from everything physicists had learned before. People coming fresh to this today are lucky. They don't have to "unlearn" the old ideas first, and that makes it much easier to describe both these big ideas in simple language for beginners.

There is no evidence that time travel *can* be achieved at present. Since the end of the 1980s, however, physicists have known that there is nothing within the general theory of relativity that forbids it. They say that whatever is not impossible, must be possible. In the words used by Conan Doyle's fictional detective Sherlock Holmes, once you eliminate the impossible, whatever remains, however improbable, must be the truth. Or as physicists put it, *what isn't forbidden is compulsory.*

So what laws of physics would allow a time machine to exist? Physicists can't yet build time machines, so they investigate the possibilities with mathematical 'models'. The model they have studied most intensively is the "wormhole" – a tunnel through space and time connecting different regions of the Universe. The idea is familiar from many science fiction stories, such as *Star Trek*, but it isn't just fiction. According to the general theory of relativity, different places really can connect through such tunnels. But so can different times – the two "mouths" of the wormhole could be next to each other in space but separated in time. It could literally be used as a time tunnel.

But you can't just pop out to the shed and build a time machine. It would involve manipulating black holes each with many times the mass of the Sun, and that would need a lot of energy. One exciting possibility is that such time machines could occur naturally. More fantastically, some scientists think that it might be possible to make tiny time tunnels, much smaller than an **atom**, and use a natural process to "inflate" them up to a human size without using much energy at all. There is at least one more way to build a time machine; we will describe all these possibilities.

Of course, if we ever did make, or find, a human-sized time machine this would raise the possibility of problems involving paradoxes. Such paradoxes are familiar from science fiction stories. The most famous is the so-called "granny paradox", where a traveller could go back in time and accidentally kill her

granny, so that her mother wouldn't ever be born, so that the time traveller would never be born, so granny would *not* be killed, and so on. This is where **quantum physics** comes in. The law that makes light travel in straight lines is a key part of quantum physics, and it is the same law that prevents time-travel paradoxes. On the other hand, as we shall also explain, it might be possible to have your cake *and* eat it – granny can be both dead and alive at the same time.

How do we know this? It all comes down to mathematics, but we won't go into the equations in this book, we'll just tell you the results of the calculations. As far as science is concerned, our journey begins in 1905, when Albert Einstein came up with his special theory of relativity, which is even easier to understand than the general theory. But as far as time travel is concerned, the journey began ten years earlier, in 1895, when H. G. Wells came up with a story that paved the way for hundreds more time travel stories, and even included one of the key ideas in what became the special theory of relativity. That story was, of course, *The Time Machine*.

Chapter 1

Elastic Time

Many people think that Albert Einstein was the first person to come up with the idea of time as the fourth dimension. But they are wrong. Einstein wasn't even the second person to come up with the idea. The first person was H. G. Wells, who published it in his book *The Time Machine* ten years before Einstein published his **special theory of relativity**. Wells has his character, the Time Traveller, explain the idea to some friends:

There is no difference between Time and any of the three dimensions of Space except that our consciousness moves along it ...

It is simply this. That Space, as our mathematicians have it, is spoken of as having three dimensions, which one may call Length, Breadth, and Thickness, and is always definable by reference to three planes, each at right angles to the

others. But some philosophical people have been asking why
three dimensions particularly – why not another direction at
right angles to the other three?

    H. G. Wells suggests, through the voice of his character,
that this fourth dimension might be what we perceive as time.

    But before we start thinking about travelling in time, we need
to be clear about what we mean by travelling in space. The
three dimensions Wells talks about correspond to our everyday
ideas of moving forward and back, left and right, or up and
down. You can get to anywhere in the Universe by a
combination of these three kinds of move, if you have the
patience for a long enough journey. That's why we say that
space is three-dimensional.

Mapping Space and Time

Physicists and mathematicians represent points in space by
coordinates, just like the way a point on a graph can be
specified by two numbers: its distance along the x-axis, and its
distance up the y-axis. You can imagine a graph in which there
are three axes at right angles to each other, representing the x,
y, and z directions. Any point in space can be specified by three
numbers, called coordinates, corresponding to the distances
along each of these axes.

There is nothing particularly deep about this. We all use this coordinate system, without realising it. If you tell a friend that you will meet her at the building on the corner of High Street and Broad Street, you are using two coordinates, corresponding to two dimensions. If you say you will meet her in the coffee shop on the second floor of that building, you are using three dimensions, because now you have included the height. And if you say you will meet her at 3 o'clock in the coffee shop on the second floor of the building on the corner of High Street and Broad Street, you have included a fourth dimension – time. But *where* is the time dimension? Wells said that it is simply a direction at right angles to *each* of the three *x*, *y*, and *z* directions. That's easy enough to say, but what does it mean?

The way the Time Traveller in the story explains it, what we see as a solid object in three-dimensional space, such as a cube, really extends in time as well – in this case, like a long, square-sided snake. Its dimensions are length, breadth, height, and something called *duration*. According to this image, a person is also like an oddly shaped worm extending through time, weaving its way past every point in space the person ever visits. Our consciousness moves along the worm from the time of our birth to the time of our death. The Time Machine that gives Wells' story its title travels forward and back along the time dimension.

What happens if somebody walks through the space where the Time Machine is whizzing along the time dimension into the future? H. G. Wells has a clever idea to answer that problem. He says that "the thinning out of matter at high speed renders the Time Traveller invisible and invulnerable", as long as he keeps moving.

The snag with all this is that if time really is like that then nothing we can do can influence the future (let alone the past). Everything exists in all four dimensions, and even the Time Traveller's adventures in the future are already fixed and predetermined before he sets out on his journey. All that happens is that his conscious awareness moves along the time trail through the adventures before coming home – almost as if it were one of the adventure rides in a theme park. But this is not the way scientists today think about time. Instead of seeing the future as fixed and inevitable, they have gone to the other extreme. They see it as not just changeable but unpredictable, so that we can never be quite sure what will happen next. Some physicists think that it may even be possible to change the past.

A Special Theory

It really was Albert Einstein who was the first person to realise that time is flexible, and can be stretched and squeezed. He discovered that time is elastic, although even he didn't realise just how much time might be affected by circumstances.

Einstein was 26 in 1905, when he came up with the idea that became the special theory of relativity by thinking about the nature of light. The name "special theory" is a bit confusing, because today we don't usually use the word "special" in quite the same way. His theory describes what happens to things when they move around, but it only deals with things moving in straight lines at constant speeds and their behaviour relative to one another. This is a "special case" of a theory – one Einstein still hadn't worked out in 1905 – that would describe the relationships between things moving in wiggly paths and changing their speed as they did so. So it became known as the special theory of relativity. When Einstein did discover the more general theory, it became known, logically enough, as the general theory of relativity. We describe that in the next chapter, because it is the theory that opens the way to time travel.

Einstein was puzzled about the nature of light. He was trying to imagine what the world would look like if you could fly along at the speed of light (300 million metres per second). What would you see if you held a mirror up in front of your face? If you were travelling as fast as light, the light reflected off your face would never be able to catch up with the mirror, so you would see no reflection in the mirror! But Einstein knew that in the nineteenth century a Scottish physicist called James Clerk Maxwell had found a set of equations that described the behaviour of light; and Einstein realised that those equations said that his imaginary idea of flying along at the speed of light was impossible.

The Speed of Light

Maxwell was interested in electricity and magnetism. In the nineteenth century he discovered a set of equations that described everything that was known about electricity and magnetism, and showed that light is a form of electricity and magnetism combined in what are called electromagnetic fields. Light is a kind of electromagnetic wave. Radio waves, microwaves, X-rays and so on are all different kinds of electromagnetic wave, but with different wavelengths.

After Maxwell's discovery, people naturally thought of these waves as something like waves on the sea, or ripples in a pond, or like sound waves travelling through the air. After all, the waves surely had to move through something. People thought that the speed of the waves needed to be measured relative to that something, just as the speed of sound is measured relative to the air or steel or whatever material it is moving through. So they thought that the whole Universe must be filled with a kind of invisible sea, which they called "the aether", and that light and other electromagnetic waves were ripples moving through the aether.

But the aether would have to have some very strange properties. **Maxwell's equations** tell us how fast electromagnetic waves are moving. The equations say that all electromagnetic waves, including light, move at the same speed. This is known as the speed of light, and it is an impressive 299.792458 million metres per second, or in round numbers 300 million metres per second, which is 300,000 km/sec. One reason people were so impressed by Maxwell's discovery is that this is exactly the speed of light measured in experiments, so they knew his equations must be right. But they also knew that the speed waves move at depends on how stiff the stuff they are moving through is. Sound waves, for example, travel much faster along a steel rod than they do through air, or through water. In order for light to travel at 300 million metres per second, the aether would have to be much, much stiffer than steel. And yet, the Earth and everything else in the Universe seemed to be able to move through the aether (through "empty space") without being affected at all!

There was another puzzle. If the Earth is moving through the aether, and light waves are moving through the aether, the speed we measure for light ought to depend on which direction the light is coming from.

If you are in a car moving at 60 km per hour past a car going the other way at 60 km per hour, your speed relative to the other car is 120 km per hour. If one car is going at 100 km per hour on the motorway and the car behind is going at 90 km per hour, the speed of the first car is 10 km per hour relative to the second car. So if we, on Earth, are following the same direction as the light waves, we expect to measure our speed as a bit less than 300 million metres per second. If we are heading straight towards the light waves, we expect to measure our speed as a bit more than 300 million metres per second. But careful experiments showed that the way the Earth was moving had no effect on the measured speed of light. It always came out as exactly 299.792458 million metres per second, at any time of day or night on the spinning Earth, and at any time of year as the Earth moves round the Sun.

This was a major mystery until Einstein came along. His

great idea was to realise that everybody was wrong about the way velocities add up. He said that people had to get rid of the idea of the aether, and accept what Maxwell's equations actually said, but that nobody before him had really believed – that the speed of light is the same no matter how fast the person who measures that speed is moving. This meant changing people's ideas about space and time, and the way velocities add up. It meant that both space and time must be *elastic* because measuring how fast people and things move involves both space and time: metres per second, miles per hour, and so on.

The Ultimate Constant

Light moves at 300 million metres per second. Einstein showed that the differences in the rules governing the speed of light are only really noticeable if things are moving at huge speeds that are a big proportion of the speed of light. The old way of adding up velocities works fine if you are comparing the speeds of cars, or planes. If you are in a car travelling at 50 km per hour and you are overtaken by a car travelling at 70 km per hour that car's speed relative to you will be just 20 km per hour. But if you have your headlights on, the speed of the light from the headlamps is 300 million metres per second relative to your car no matter how fast you are driving. It will also be 300 million metres per second relative to the other car, or to anybody else. And light does not need the aether to travel through, because the magnetic and electric parts of the electromagnetic wave push each other along through space, once energy has been put in (for example, from the hot filaments in a lamp) to set them moving.

This makes the speed of light an absolute constant. It is the most important natural constant there is, so it is referred to by the letter *c*, the first letter of the word "constant".

Stretching Time and Squeezing Space

Einstein found a set of equations that describe, among other things, how velocities add up if the speed of light is always c, no matter who measures it and how they are moving. The equations show that adding up two velocities *always* gives you a total that is less than the speed of light.

For example, if a spaceship is moving away at 0.75*c* relative to the Earth and fires a smaller rocket out forwards at 0.75*c* relative to the spaceship, the speed of that rocket relative to the Earth will *not* be 1.5*c*, but 0.96*c*.

So nothing can ever be accelerated to a speed faster than the speed of light. It is the ultimate speed limit. This is because both space and time, two components of **velocity**, are distorted by motion. (Velocity is a measure of both the speed – time and space – an object is moving at, *and the direction it is moving in*.)

If a spaceship really was moving past you at 0.75*c*, time would run more slowly in the spaceship than it does for you. This is literally true; it is not some kind of illusion. Even more strangely, any astronaut on board the spaceship is entitled to say that they are standing still, and that you are moving past at 0.75*c*, so that your clock is running slow. This is an extreme example of how the way we observe our surroundings is "relative" to where we make the observations and how we are moving.

We are mainly interested in twisting time in this book, so we can show how this works by looking at how time is measured. Because *c* is the ultimate constant, the best and

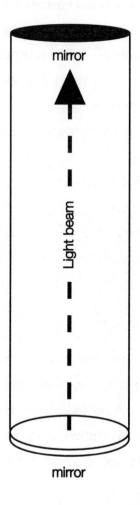

mirror

Light beam

mirror

most accurate way to measure time is in terms of how long it takes light to travel a certain distance. The ideal clock would be two perfect mirrors opposite one another with a light beam bouncing between them. Each time the beam hits one of the mirrors, that corresponds to one tick of the clock.

If you are in the spaceship, with your mirror clock stationary, each tick of the clock corresponds to the time it takes for the light to travel straight up and down between the mirrors. But if your spaceship is moving past us at high speed, the way we see it the whole setup moves along while the light is moving up and down, so the light has to travel along two sides of a triangle to get back to where it started.

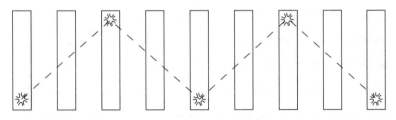

Moving light clock

This is a longer distance, so it takes a longer time. We see your moving clock running slower. And you would see our clocks running slower in exactly the same way! This is called **time dilation**. It applies to all kinds of ways of measuring time, not just light clocks.

Testing Einstein

Length contraction is harder to imagine, but it is just as real. In four dimensions, the amount by which length shrinks and time stretches for a moving object cancel each other out. This balancing act has been seen at work in real experiments that have been carried out in particle accelerators, machines which shoot beams of particles down long tunnels at close to the speed of light. Some of these particles, which are much smaller than atoms, have very short lifetimes before they "decay" and turn into other particles. A typical particle might have a lifetime of one ten-millionth of a second. Travelling at the speed of light, if there were no time dilation effect the particle could travel only 30 metres before it decayed. If it moved at 12/13 of the speed of light, which is the sort of speed reached in such experiments, common sense says it could only travel 12/13ths of 30 metres, which is 27.7 metres. But using Einstein's formula for the time dilation effect, at that speed the particle would have a lifetime stretched so much that it would travel 2.6 times as far, a distance of just over 72 metres. Sure enough, experiments with such particles show they can reach targets exactly the "extra" distance down the tunnels that the special theory predicts.

But everything is supposed to be relative. How does it look

from the point of view of the particle? From that point of view, the whole world is rushing by at $^{12}/_{13}c$, and the particle is standing still. In which case the tube is *shrunk*, by exactly the same amount, 2.6 times, and even though the particle only lives for one ten-millionth of a second it still gets 72 per cent of the way down the tunnel!

This is always the case. Observers moving at different velocities each have their own view of the Universe and their own ideas about which clocks are running slow and how space has been shrunk. But they almost always agree in their measurements of things that are at the same time and place. There is one important exception. That exception opens the door to a kind of one-way time travel.

One-Way Time Travel

The best way to picture what is going on is to imagine what the world looks like to two twin sisters, one of whom goes on a long journey at a very high speed, a large proportion of the speed of light, while the other one stays at home. Of course, we don't just imagine what will happen; we can calculate exactly what will happen, using Einstein's equations – the same equations that have been proved right in every experiment carried out since 1905, including the experiments with particles being sent down long tubes at high speeds. As long as the travelling twin keeps on travelling at a constant speed in a straight line, which is just what we mean by constant velocity, everything is symmetrical. Each twin is entitled to say that she is standing still, or "at rest", and the other twin is moving. Each twin will say that the other twin's clocks are running slow.

But what happens when the travelling twin turns round and comes home? The crucial thing is that only one of the twins turns round. She changes her velocity, just about as dramatically as it is possible to change velocity, by going back

in the opposite direction from the one she was going in at first. This destroys the symmetry, and now we can definitely say which one of the twins is the traveller and which one has not been on a journey. Time runs more slowly for the travelling twin than for her sister, and when she gets home she will be younger than her sister.

The travelling twin will find that time has passed faster back home than in her spaceship, so she will have travelled into the future. This is literally true; it is not just that her clocks have been running slow in the sense that they are not working properly. Time itself runs more slowly for the travelling twin. But the travelling twin's time journey could only be one way, to the future – the special theory of relativity does not tell us how to travel backwards in time.

Once again, this has been proved by experiments. If two identical particles with identical lifetimes are made in an experiment in a laboratory, but one of them is sent on a circular path at very high speeds round a circular particle accelerator, it will get back to its starting place with more of its lifetime left than if it had stood still. The moving particle ages more slowly than its partner.

It is easy to accelerate particles to very high speeds, but very difficult to accelerate spaceships, let alone human beings, to speeds close to the speed of light. But if we ignore the practical difficulties, what do the equations tell us?

In order to see how one-way time travel might work, we have to learn to think in terms of very large distances, as well as very high speeds. Remember that the speed of light is near enough 300,000 km per second. At that enormous speed, in one year light travels just under 9.5 million million kilometres. This distance is known as a **light year**. To put it in perspective, the nearest star to the Sun is 4.3 light years away. So light literally takes 4.3 years to travel the distance from that star, Proxima Centauri, to us. A light year is a measure of *distance*, not of time, and even a light year is a short distance by astronomical standards.

With that in mind, imagine that the travelling twin goes on a voyage covering 25 light years each way, at 98 per cent of the speed of light. According to the clocks and calendars back on Earth, the journey will take 51 years. The stay-at-home twin will be 51 years older when her sister returns. But according to all the clocks and calendars on the spaceship, the journey will only take 10 years! The travelling twin will only be 10 years older when she returns home. She will be 41 years younger than her sister, and as far as she is concerned she will have travelled 51 years into the future while only living through 10 years. For longer voyages, she would travel even farther into the future. This is an idea which has been taken up by several science fiction writers; author Larry Niven uses it very well in many of his stories. But it isn't just science fiction. The Universe really does work like that.

The Geometry of Relativity

When people talk about time travel, though, what they are usually interested in is travelling into the past – if only in order to come back from the future, like H. G. Wells' Traveller, to tell their friends about their adventures. After all, we already travel into the future, at a steady rate of 60 minutes every hour, and 24 hours every day. But we cannot go back even one second. Or can we?

The key to opening a door into the past comes from Einstein's second great theory, the **general theory of relativity**. And the best way to understand it is with the help of the second person to come up with the idea of time as the fourth dimension, a mathematics professor called Hermann Minkowski. He was one of Einstein's teachers when Einstein was a student in Zurich at the end of the 1890s.

In fact, Minkowski had not been very impressed by the young Albert Einstein, who was 17 when he started his university course in Zurich in 1896. Minkowski described him as "a lazy dog who never bothered about mathematics at all". But Minkowski was one of the first people who really understood the special theory of relativity. He understood it so well that he came up with a clear way of explaining it, or describing it, that even Einstein hadn't thought of.

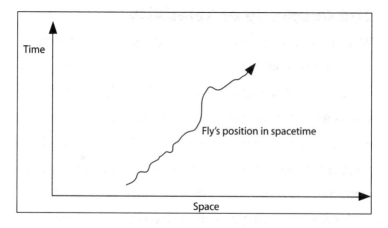

It all comes back to coordinates. Think of a fly buzzing round a room. At any instant in time, you can specify exactly where the fly is in terms of its distance from the ceiling and from two of the walls that meet in a corner – in terms of three coordinates. Minkowski realised that you can also specify the entire life history of the fly in terms of *four* coordinates – the three spatial coordinates plus one of time. It's difficult to visualise four dimensions, so mathematicians

23

like Minkowski imagine compressing all of space into one dimension, represented by the horizontal axis on a graph, and representing time using the vertical axis on the graph. Such graphs are called "**spacetime diagrams**", or, in his honour, "**Minkowski diagrams**". If a particle (or a fly) moves about in space as time passes, it makes a wiggly line on the Minkowski diagram. You can look up the vertical axis to any time you choose and then across the diagram to read off the position of the fly at that time.

In principle, you could do the same thing with a four-dimensional graph, if you could draw in four dimensions. As Minkowski put it, in a lecture he gave in 1908:

Henceforth space by itself, and time by itself, are doomed to fade into mere shadows, and only a kind of union of the two will preserve an independent reality.

We can see what he meant by thinking about the way a drum-majorette's mace changes its appearance as it is tossed, twirling, into the air.

The mace is a solid, three-dimensional object which has a definite length. But depending on your point of view – your perspective – as it twirls through the air it may show its full length, if you are viewing it from the side, or hardly any length at all, if you are viewing it almost end-on, or any length in between.

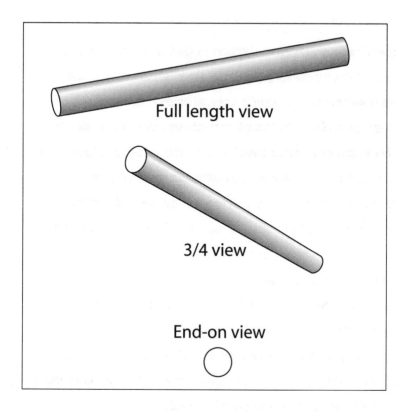

Full length view

3/4 view

End-on view

The changes are caused by the way the mace is moving in three dimensions. In the same way, all the strange features of the special theory of relativity, including **length contraction** and stretching time, can be explained in terms of the way things move in four dimensions. Just as the mace has a fixed length in three dimensions, objects have a fixed size in four dimensions. This is called **extension**.

A particular four-dimensional extension corresponds to the

movement of an object through three-dimensional space at a particular velocity for a particular time. Einstein's discovery of the way *moving clocks run slow* while *moving rulers shrink* describes the same sort of perspective effect as the twirling mace, but operating in the four dimensions of spacetime. Although both time and three-dimensional length are distorted by motion, there is a "four-dimensional length" which stays the same.

Motion makes space shrink, but it makes time expand. So time cannot be just a fourth dimension of space, the way H. G. Wells described it. In Einstein's equations the symbol representing time (*the time parameter*) has a minus sign in front of it, while all three dimensions of space have plus signs. So time is a kind of negative space – which is why it is affected in the opposite way by motion. That is why the time and space effects cancel each other out and leave the extension unchanged. And in those equations, time is always multiplied by the speed of light, so that **one second of time** is equivalent to **300,000 km of space**. That is why relativistic effects only become obvious for things moving at a large proportion of the speed of light.

This is what makes life difficult for would-be time travellers. Imagine you had a machine like the one in H. G. Wells' story, which could somehow rotate itself through the dimensions and line itself up so that one of the space directions actually became the time direction. Perhaps the "forward-back" direction of space might get swapped with the "future-past" direction of time. You might imagine that then you could travel into the past simply by moving the time machine backwards for a certain distance, then rotating back into the usual dimensions of space. But in order to travel back one second in time, you would have to travel 300,000 km along this time direction. To go back a year into the past, you would have to travel a light year in length. You would still need an incredibly fast spaceship to get to any interesting times in the distant past.

The Relativity of Geometry

All of the mathematical models show that when scientists say that time is the fourth dimension, they are right, but it doesn't follow exactly the same rules as the three dimensions of space. Even so, Minkowski's idea of spacetime did make it possible to describe the special theory of relativity in terms of geometry. All mathematicians understand geometry, so this made the special theory much easier for them to understand and to work with.

One of the best known ideas in geometry is Pythagoras' theorem. This theorem says that the sum of the squares of the lengths of the two sides of a right-angle triangle that meet in the right angle is equal to the square of the length of the other side, the hypotenuse. Four-dimensional extension is related to the three dimensions of space and one of time in exactly the same way, through a kind of four-dimensional Pythagoras' theorem. Extension is the hypotenuse, and the square of its "length" is equal to the sum of the squares of three space lengths, *minus* the square of the appropriate time duration. For mathematicians, this makes it very easy to understand and work with the equations. It also makes it easy to see why the "special" theory (see page 9) really is a special case.

Pythagoras' theorem is exactly true for triangles drawn on a flat sheet of paper, or on any flat surface. On a *flat* surface, the angles of a triangle always add up to exactly 180 degrees. But neither of those things are true on a *curved* surface, like the surface of a sphere. It isn't even always clear what you mean by "the hypotenuse" for triangles drawn on the surface of a sphere. On a sphere, you can even draw triangles in which all three of the angles are right angles, so every side is an hypotenuse and the total of the angles adds up to 270 degrees! On the surface of a sphere the angles of a triangle always add up to more than 180 degrees. In principle, if you didn't know that the Earth was round, you could find out by drawing huge triangles on some

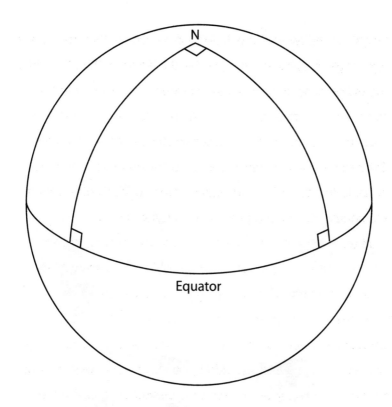

large empty desert and measuring the angles.

The surface of a sphere, like the Earth, is said to be "closed", because it bends back on itself. There is no edge, but the surface has a definite area. If you set out in one direction on a closed surface and keep going you will end up back where you started, after travelling right round the surface.

There is another kind of geometry which works on a different kind of curved surface – the kind that is said to be "open". It is harder to picture than the surface of a sphere, but it is a bit like the shape of a saddle, or a mountain pass. The most important thing about the geometry of an open surface is that the angles of a triangle always add up to *less* than 180 degrees.

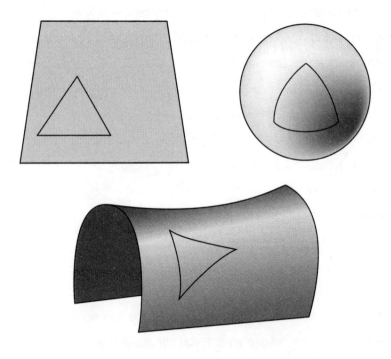

An open surface in the real world has to have an edge, and be a definite size, because it can't be infinitely big; but mathematicians happily play with equations that describe open surfaces that don't have an edge, but go on for ever in all directions. On a surface like that if you set out in one direction and kept going for ever you would never reach an edge and would always pass through new places, never getting back to where you started.

A *flat* surface is a special case, exactly on the border between being open and being closed. Minkowski's spacetime geometry is also a special case, a four-dimensional geometry on the border between "open" and "closed" four-dimensional geometries. Just as the surface of the Earth, or the surface of a saddle, can be curved, so spacetime itself can be curved. And although Einstein didn't actually use geometry to discover the general theory of relativity, the best way to understand the general theory, and the way it opens the door to time travel, is in terms of curved spacetime.

Albert Einstein (1879-1955)

Albert Einstein was born at Ulm, in Germany, on 14 March 1879. When he was still a baby, his family moved to Munich, where he went to school. When he was five years old, Albert had to stay in bed because he was ill and his father gave him a magnetic compass to play with. This was better than anything he had ever seen before and Albert was fascinated by the mysterious way in which the compass needle always pointed to the north. He wondered why he'd never been shown anything that interesting in school. Albert Einstein hated every school he ever went to and would much rather have stayed at home working on puzzles that interested him.

In 1894, when Albert was just 15, his family moved to Italy, where his father started an electricity business. But Albert was told to stay in Munich on his own to complete his education. At least, that was the idea. Within six months, he persuaded his doctor to write a letter to the school saying that Albert was suffering so much stress being on his own that he had to leave and join his parents and sister in Italy.

After a year swanning around Italy and having a good time, Albert tried to enrol at the technical university in

Zurich, known as the ETH, but failed the entrance examination. He had to spend a year catching up with his studies in a Swiss school before he got in to the ETH in 1896. There, he was a dreadful student who didn't bother going to lectures, but he read a lot and discussed new scientific ideas with his friends. He also met a fellow student, Mileva Maric, who he eventually married.

Although Einstein crammed for his final examinations by borrowing a friend's lecture notes to study, he didn't get a very good degree, so he couldn't stay at the university to get a PhD. He had to get a job, eventually settling down at the patent office in Bern in 1902. It was while he was working as a patent officer that he carried out his work on, among other things, the special theory of relativity. He also managed to complete a PhD in 1905. But it wasn't until 1909 that he left the patent office and became a professor at Zurich.

Over the following years, Einstein worked at several universities before settling in Berlin, where he completed his work on the general theory of relativity. His first marriage ended in a bitter divorce, and in 1919, the year he turned 40, Einstein married his cousin Elsa, who had also been married before. Although his greatest work was *behind him by then, Einstein travelled the world describing his ideas, and made important contributions to quantum physics.*

After Hitler came to power in 1933, the Einsteins, who were Jewish, had to leave Germany for good, and settled in the United States. Elsa died in 1936, and for the rest of

his life Einstein lived in Princeton, working at the Institute for Advanced Study and becoming the white-haired old man who most people think of as soon as they hear the word "scientist". The character Emmett "Doc" Brown in the **Back to the Future** movies is clearly based on this archetypal image of Einstein. But when he did his great work, Einstein was actually a handsome young man with dark hair.

Chapter 2

Cosmic Connections

Even when he was working out the special theory of relativity, Einstein knew that it was just the first step towards a general theory. The general theory of relativity would have to take account of how the world looks to things that change their velocity – things that are accelerated. Because velocity is a measure of both the speed and the direction in which an object is moving, acceleration can involve a change in speed, or a change in direction, or both. If you turn a corner, you are accelerating, even if you keep going at a steady speed.

It took Einstein ten years, from 1905 to 1915, to get from the special theory to the general theory. Einstein's inspiration for the special theory was his image of what the world would look like if you could fly at the speed of light. His inspiration for the general theory was an image of how the world would appear to somebody trapped in a falling lift.

Einstein imagined that the cable had snapped, all the safety devices had failed, and the lift was falling completely freely, with no effects of friction. Both the lift and the people in it would be accelerated by the gravitational pull of the Earth, moving faster and faster as they fell. But Einstein realised that because the lift and everything in it would be affected in exactly the same way, all falling together, the people inside would float about as if **gravity** did not exist. It would be exactly the same for them as if the lift were floating in space, so far from any star or planet it wouldn't be affected by gravity.

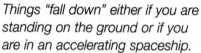

Things "fall down" either if you are standing on the ground or if you are in an accelerating spaceship.

Einstein realised that acceleration can cancel out the effects of gravity. Or as he put it, "for a man falling from a roof, gravity does not exist." What he meant was, the falling man would feel as if he was floating. This is easy for us to accept, because we have all seen images of astronauts floating about in their spaceships. The astronauts and their spaceship are all in orbit around the Earth, being accelerated in the same way as they fall (remember, a change of direction is acceleration) with gravity cancelled out. But it was a great leap of imagination for Einstein a century ago.

He also realised that the effect would work the other way

round. If something pushed the lift with a constant acceleration, the effect on the people inside the lift would be as if gravity was at work and their weight had returned. This happens to astronauts when their rockets take off. On a much smaller scale you can experience the same effect when you are in an accelerating car, or when a lift starts moving upwards. But Einstein was the first person to realise that gravity and acceleration are equivalent to one another. In everyday language, they are the same. This meant that the general theory Einstein was looking for had to describe gravity, as well as accelerated motion.

Bending Light

That set Einstein thinking about light again. Now, he imagined that there might be a tiny hole in one side of the falling lift, and that a light ray came in through the hole. If the lift really was floating freely in space, the light ray would travel across the lift in a straight line to hit the opposite wall exactly level with the hole. If the lift was falling, you might guess the light ought to make a spot on the opposite wall a little higher up than the hole it came in through. This would correspond to the distance the lift had fallen while the light was crossing it. So if everything in the falling lift really behaved as if it were floating freely in space, the only way that the

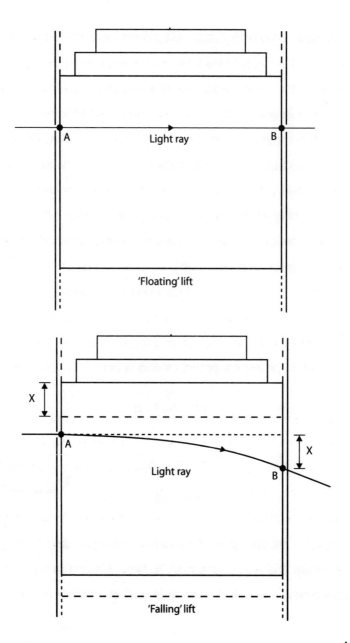

'Floating' lift

Light ray

A

B

X

X

Light ray

A

B

'Falling' lift

light beam could hit the other wall exactly opposite the hole it came in by would be if the light beam was bent downwards by gravity exactly the right distance as it crossed the lift.

From this simple insight, Einstein was able to find the equations of the general theory of relativity. He realised that he could use them to calculate, among other things, how strongly gravity affects light. Einstein worked out how much a light ray from a distant star would be bent as it went past the edge of the Sun.

The effect could only be measured during an eclipse, when the blinding light from the Sun is blocked out by the Moon, so the stars beyond the edge of the Sun can be seen and photographed. Just such an eclipse happened in 1919. The light bending effect was measured, and found to be exactly what Einstein had predicted, proving the idea of curved spacetime.

The light-bending effect of the Sun's gravity

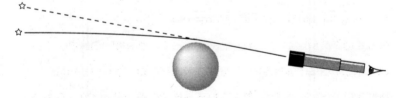

But it's still easier for us to think about space and time separately. The kind of geometry Minkowski used to describe spacetime is equivalent to the geometry of triangles drawn on a flat sheet of paper. But the geometry that explains light bending is equivalent to the geometry of triangles drawn on a curved surface. Einstein realised that it is possible that space itself is curved.

This isn't "just common sense" because on a large scale the curvature is too small to notice. On the surface of the Earth the curvature is not observable in everyday life as we are living on the surface of such a large sphere. The sphere is big and the curvature is small. Astronomers have discovered that the curvature of the Universe is also very small. It's so small that it can't be measured. As far as we can tell, overall space is in fact flat.

There are many ways in which astronomers can tell this. One of the simplest is equivalent to drawing large triangles in the desert and measuring the size of their angles. The area of a circle with radius r drawn on a flat piece of paper is πr^2. In flat space (a flat Universe) the volume of a sphere with radius r is equal to $\frac{4}{3}\pi r^3$. In curved space, the volume of a sphere can be bigger or smaller than this, depending on the curvature being closed or open. This is just like the way that on a curved surface the angles of a triangle may add up to more or less than 180 degrees, depending on the curvature.

There are islands of stars called galaxies spread out more or less evenly through space, so astronomers can measure the volumes of spheres of different sizes by counting the numbers of galaxies in the spheres. The numbers they get match what they expect for a flat Universe. There are more accurate methods of measuring the flatness of space, but they are harder to understand in everyday terms. The important thing is that every measurement shows that the Universe is flat, in a three-dimensional sense.

This makes it easier to work with the equations of the general theory of relativity when they are applied to the real Universe, and to describe how things behave in the real Universe. In particular, it makes it easy to understand how gravity bends light. It happens because in some places there are dents in the flat Universe.

Bending Space

When we see light being bent, what is actually being bent is space itself. Things make dents in space; the more mass something has the bigger the dent. An easy way to picture this is to imagine the smooth, stretched surface of a trampoline. This is like flat space. Now imagine a heavy bowling ball placed on the trampoline. It will make a dent, corresponding to curved space. If the ball wasn't there, you could roll a marble across the trampoline and it would travel in a straight line. But if the bowling ball is there, when you roll a marble past the ball it will follow the dent and go in a slightly curved path. It is the dent in space made by the Sun that is responsible for the curved path followed by light rays grazing the surface of the Sun. But even though the Sun is 330,000 times more massive than the Earth, it has only enough gravity to make a barely noticeable dent in space.

The Sun is an ordinary star, which looks so bright to us only because it is much closer than the other stars. So everything we can say about the way the Sun bends spacetime also applies to other stars.

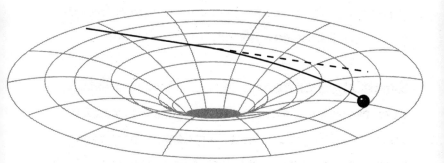

The paths followed by light rays in curved space are the equivalent of straight lines in flat space. The paths followed by light rays in any kind of curved space are called **geodesics**;

straight lines in flat space are a special kind of geodesic.

The more mass there is piled up in one place in space, the bigger the dent it makes in space, and the more the geodesics are curved. If the dent becomes deep-enough, the geodesics along which light rays travel get bent right back on themselves, and cannot escape out into the Universe. The massive object has become a **black hole**.

"Discovering" Black Holes

Einstein announced the discovery of the general theory of relativity in November 1915. Almost immediately, a German astronomer called Karl Schwarzschild used the equations to work out how much space is bent around different kinds of object. He discovered that if any amount of matter is squeezed into a small enough space, its gravity will bend light back on itself to make a black hole. Schwarzschild had "discovered" black holes just by using mathematics, although the name "black hole" was only given to these objects in 1967, by the American John Wheeler.

The simplest way to picture what Schwarzschild had discovered is to imagine squeezing any object – any mass – into a ball. If the radius of the ball is smaller than a certain amount, the object becomes a black hole with a gravitational pull from which nothing can escape. This special radius for any particular mass is now known as the **Schwarzschild radius**. The Schwarzschild radius is the radius of the black hole.

The Schwarzschild radius for the Earth is 0.88 cm, not much bigger than a large pea. This doesn't mean that there is a black hole with a radius of 0.88 cm sitting in the centre of the Earth. It means that if the entire Earth could be squeezed inside that radius, the gravity of that concentration of mass would be so strong that it would bend space right round on itself and cut the pea-sized black hole off from the Universe outside.

The bigger the amount of mass involved, the bigger the Schwarzschild radius. The Schwarzschild radius for the Sun is 2.9 km. If the Sun could be squeezed into a ball 2.9 km across, it would cut itself off from the world outside, and become a black hole from which nothing could escape.

There is another way to imagine making a black hole. Instead of squeezing something like the Sun into a tiny volume, you could add more and more matter to make it bigger and increase its gravitational pull. If there was a star five hundred times bigger than our Sun, but with the same density as the Sun, it would be about the same distance across as our Solar System from the Sun out to the orbit of Pluto. The density of this superstar would only be about one-and-a-half times the density of water, but space would be completely bent around the huge object, so it could not be seen from outside. It would be a black hole.

You could make a black hole out of water, if you had enough of it. Of course, such an object could not really exist. It would be crushed by its own weight and all the matter would fall in to the centre. So the whole idea of black holes sounded crazy when Schwarzschild first came up with it. Most scientists thought there must be a law of nature which stopped such things happening. Then, they discovered stars which are on the very edge of collapsing to make black holes.

Towards the Black Hole

A star like the Sun keeps shining because nuclear energy is released deep inside it. This energy is released when hydrogen is converted into helium. It is exactly the same as the way energy is released in a hydrogen bomb; stars are like huge hydrogen bombs that explode for billions of years. The heat produced inside the Sun in this way makes a pressure which holds the rest of the Sun up. That is why the Sun is about a hundred times bigger in diameter than the Earth is, even though it is a third of a million times more massive than the Earth, and gravity is trying to squeeze it smaller.

When all the fuel in the heart of the Sun is used up, in about five billion years' time, it will cool off inside and gravity will make it shrink. It will end up as a solid lump of star stuff, about the same size as the Earth, a dead star called a **white dwarf**. The density of a white dwarf is about a million times the density of water. One cubic centimetre of white dwarf matter would have a mass of about one tonne.

Astronomers have discovered many white dwarf stars and studied them using telescopes and spectrographs. So astronomers know that this description of the fate of a star like the Sun is correct. The instruments analyse the light from the stars and tell us what the stars are made of and what conditions are like there. A white dwarf star has a radius of 5,000 km or more, a lot bigger than the 3 km or so of the Schwarzschild radius for that much mass. If that was the end of the story, we wouldn't have to worry about black holes. But it isn't the end of the story.

In the 1930s, an Indian scientist from Lahore, Subrahmanyan Chandrasekhar, used the new ideas of quantum physics to work out what would happen to a white dwarf star with a larger mass than our Sun. He found that if a white dwarf has more than 1.4 times as much mass as the Sun, it cannot hold itself up but must collapse and shrink even more. This mass is now called the **Chandrasekhar limit**.

Most astronomers thought he must be wrong, since they didn't believe anything could shrink for ever, and they hadn't found any stars smaller than white dwarfs. They thought the equations of quantum physics must be wrong. But some physicists who liked playing with equations worked out what it would mean if Chandrasekhar was right. They worked out that if a dead star had between 1.5 and 3 times the mass of our Sun, it could shrink into a ball only about 10 km across. Such a ball of star stuff would be made almost entirely of neutrons. These are particles usually found only in the **nucleus** of an atom. So these dead stars are called **neutron stars**, and each one is like a single atomic nucleus 10 km across. Each cubic centimetre of a neutron star would have a mass of 100 million tonnes – 100 million times the density of a white dwarf.

But the equations also said that if a neutron star had a mass more than three times the mass of our Sun, its matter would be crushed by its own gravity and it would collapse right down to a point. (The point is called a **singularity**.) And along the way, it would disappear inside a black hole.

Comparing diameters, the Sun is 100 times bigger than a

Relative Sizes

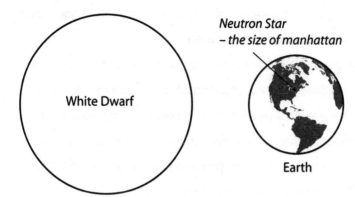

A white dwarf is 700 times bigger than a neutron star

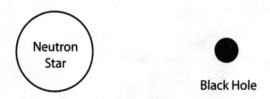

A neutron star is three times bigger than a black hole

white dwarf, and a white dwarf is 700 times bigger than a neutron star; but a neutron star is only three times bigger than a black hole. If neutron stars really exist, it would prove the equations were right and it would be hard to believe that black holes do not exist.

Neutron stars were actually discovered in the 1960s, using

radio telescopes. Many neutron stars have strong magnetic fields and spin very fast, producing beams of radio noise that whip around the sky like celestial lighthouse beams. The beams are picked up on Earth as pulses of radio noise, so these stars are known as pulsars. The discovery of pulsars proved the existence of neutron stars, and these are objects only three times bigger than black holes. In the 1960s scientists began to believe in black holes, and gave them their name. In the 1970s,

An 'invisible man' in space.

sixty years after Einstein discovered the general theory of relativity, astronomers actually discovered real black holes in space.

Black Holes Revealed

How can you see something that is invisible? In science fiction movies, an "invisible man" can be seen if he is wearing clothes, or if he picks things up and moves them about. Black holes in space can be seen when they are surrounded by hot gas and dust, and by the way their gravity affects things near to them.

A solitary black hole in space would be very difficult to find, but most stars are not alone in space. More than half of all stars have companions. The two companion stars orbit around each other like the Moon orbiting around the Earth. Because stars burn up their fuel at different rates, depending on how much mass they have, one of the two stars is bound to burn out before the other one does. If the dead star has less than 1.4 times the mass of our Sun, it will end up as a white dwarf, orbiting around the other star. If it has between 1.4 and 3 times the mass of our Sun, it will end up as a neutron star. But if it has more than three times the mass of our Sun, it will end up as a black hole.

The gravity of the black hole will tug streamers of gas away from the other star and funnel them towards the black hole. But the black hole is very small, only a few kilometres across. So the gas falling into the hole gets piled up around it in a swirling disc, like water going down the plughole of a bath. The stuff in the swirling disc gets very hot, because atoms are hitting one another and moving faster and faster as they fall in towards the centre. The gas gets so hot that it radiates energy in the form of X-rays.

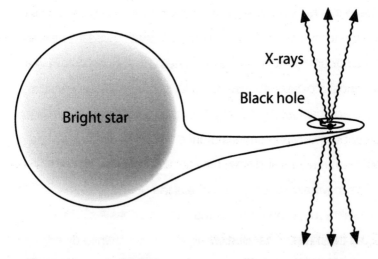

The same sort of thing can happen with a neutron star. Matter falling on to the surface of a neutron star can also get so hot that it radiates X-rays. In the 1970s, when X-ray telescopes were first launched on satellites orbiting the Earth, astronomers began to find many places where X-rays are coming from something orbiting around an ordinary bright star. At first, they couldn't tell whether the "something" was a neutron star or a black hole.

But the gravity of the companion tugs on the bright star and jiggles it from side to side. By measuring how much the companion object moves the bright star from side to side as it orbits, astronomers can work out how much mass the orbiting objects have. Many of them have as much as 8 or 10 times the mass of our Sun, and some even more. These masses are far too big for the objects to be neutron stars, so astronomers are certain that they have found black holes in space. That means we have to believe the equations that describe how space is bent around black holes. And because the equations actually describe space*time*, not just space, it means we have to believe the equations when they tell us that a black hole may be a hole in *time*, not just a hole in space.

Spacetime Tunnels

According to the general theory of relativity, everything that falls into a black hole falls all the way on to a single point at the centre, the singularity. If this were true, it would mean that all the matter inside the black hole was squeezed into zero volume, so the singularity had infinite density.

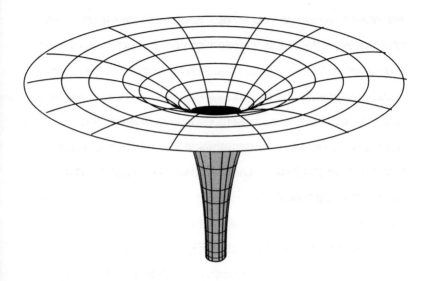

Scientists do not believe it when their equations tell them that something is infinite. They take it as a sign that there is something wrong with the equations. The general theory of relativity is the best theory of space, time and gravity that anyone has ever discovered, and it explains everything we see outside black holes; but it cannot explain what goes on right at the very heart of a black hole.

If there was a singularity at the heart of a black hole, the dent that the black hole makes in spacetime would go down to a sharp point, like an upside-down wizard's cap – like the Sorting Hat in Harry Potter. If it really is impossible for a singularity to exist, the shape of the dent would be more like that of a funnel, going down into a narrow tube, or tunnel. The tube would be the ultimate bottomless pit. It could get narrower and narrower for ever without the sides ever actually touching to make a singularity.

Or there is another possibility. What if the tunnel narrows down at first, but then opens up again into another region of space and time? Could it form a kind of "**wormhole**" joining two black holes together?

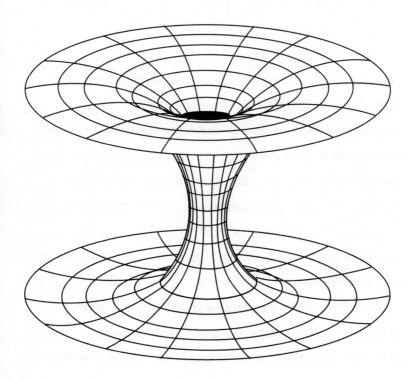

This idea isn't as crazy as it sounds. It isn't even new. Way back in 1916, an Austrian, Ludwig Flamm, realised that Schwarzschild's version of Einstein's equations actually has an inbuilt symmetry. The equations come with a mirror image. Instead of just describing a single black hole, they actually describe a tunnel connecting two black holes in different parts of flat spacetime. Einstein himself studied these equations, with his colleague Nathan Rosen. In the 1930s they found that according to the equations a wormhole could act as a bridge joining two separate universes together. This became known as an **Einstein-Rosen bridge**.

Einstein was worried about what this meant. How could there be "other universes"? When he looked at the equations more closely, Einstein discovered that in order to get through the wormhole, you would have to travel *faster* than light. Since that is impossible, there would be no way to use an Einstein-Rosen bridge to cross to another universe, or even to send messages from one universe to the other. So he decided that there was no point in worrying about what the other universes are, or where they are.

But what if a spacetime tunnel doesn't link two separate universes together, but two separate *parts* of our own Universe – our own spacetime? It would link different places together like a kind of cosmic subway, but it would also link different times together. It would be a time machine. Most scientists didn't take this idea seriously, but science fiction writers loved it. There was even a TV series called *Time Tunnel*, and the starship *Enterprise* travels through a wormhole in more than one episode of *Star Trek*.

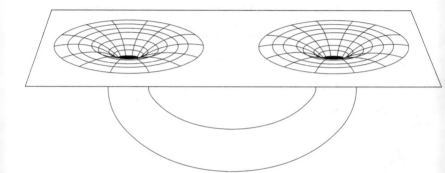

For 50 years after Einstein and Rosen came up with their idea of a bridge between universes, time tunnels remained firmly in the realm of science fiction. Then, in a curious twist, in the middle of the 1980s they left the pages of one particular science fiction story to become real science. We'll get on to that in Chapter Four.

But the science of time travel today doesn't only involve the general theory of relativity, It also takes on board the other great idea from twentieth century physics, quantum theory. Quantum physics does away with singularities and tells us how to keep wormholes open. It shows us where the other universes that Einstein worried about might be, and shows how the decisions we make really do change the future. And it also involves the most famous fictional cat in the whole of science. It's time to look at cats and quanta.

Karl Schwarzschild (1873-1916)

Karl Schwarzschild was born in Frankfurt am Main on 9 October 1873. He was the oldest of seven children, with five younger brothers and a sister. After attending primary school, he moved on to secondary school when he was eleven. There, he became very interested in astronomy, and made his own telescope. He was also very good at maths, and wrote two papers about the orbits of double stars which were published just before he was 17.

After leaving school, Schwarzschild studied at the University of Strasbourg and then at the University of Munich. He got his PhD in 1896, and found a job at an observatory in Vienna. In 1899, he went back to the University of Munich as a teacher, and a year later he investigated the idea that space might be curved. From 1901 to 1909 he was a Professor at Göttingen University, where one of his colleagues was Hermann Minkowski, who had been one of Einstein's teachers. He became the Director of the university's observatory in 1902, and got married in 1909. The Schwarschilds had three children (two boys and a girl). One of them,

Martin Schwarzschild, grew up to be a Professor of Astronomy at Princeton, in the United States.

Just after he got married, Schwarzschild was appointed to the top astronomy job in Germany, Director of the Astrophysical Laboratory in Potsdam. The Potsdam Observatory sent a team of astronomers to Tenerife, in the Canary Islands, to study the return of Halley's Comet in 1910; Schwarzschild did not go on the expedition, but he was in charge of the analysis of the photographs and other data brought back by the expedition. He would probably have stayed at Potsdam for the rest of his career, but when the First World War started in 1914 he volunteered for military service, even though he was more than 40 years old. He served in Belgium, in charge of a weather station, and in France, calculating trajectories for the artillery, before being posted to the Eastern Front, in Russia.

While he was on the Eastern Front, when he was not busy with his military duties in the artillery, Schwarzschild kept up with the scientific news from Germany. He heard about the general theory of relativity almost as soon as Einstein announced it. He worked out how the equations of the general theory describe bent space around a very dense lump of matter, and wrote two papers about what we now call black holes, which he sent back to Germany from the Eastern Front. When Einstein read the first of these two papers, he said "I had not expected that one could formulate the exact solution of the problem in such a simple way." This is now known as the Schwarzschild solution to Einstein's equations.

At the time Schwarzschild finished writing those papers, he was already suffering from pemphigus, a painful skin disease. There was no cure for the illness at the time and Schwarzschild knew that he was dying. Einstein read Schwarzschild's two papers on black holes to meetings of the Berlin Academy of sciences on 16 January and 24 February 1916. In March, Schwarzschild was brought home to Potsdam, where he died on 11 May 1916, at the age of 42.

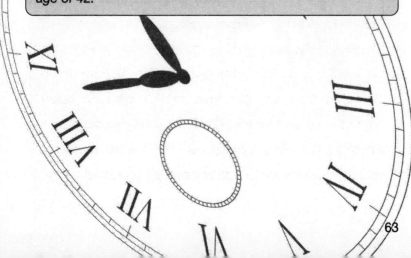

Chapter 3

The Cat and the Quantum

Some scientific expressions become part of everyday language. The term "black hole" is used to refer to any kind of bottomless pit, and that's more or less right. The term **"quantum leap"** is usually used to refer to a very big change, but that's completely wrong. The important thing about a quantum leap is that it is the smallest change it is possible to make. A quantum leap is something that happens to things like atoms, when they change from one state to another and there is nothing in between the two states.

If a ball rolls down a smooth slope, like a hill or a playground slide, it could stop anywhere at all down the slope. Each point on the slope is a different height above the ground, and that means it corresponds to a different amount of gravitational energy. When things fall down, or roll down a slope, **gravitational energy** gets turned into their energy of motion, called **kinetic energy**. That's why atoms of gas falling into a black hole move fast and get hot.

The energy of the ball on the slide changes smoothly as it rolls down. But what happens to a ball on a staircase? Each step on the staircase corresponds to a certain energy, with no in-between energy levels. A quantum leap is like the ball disappearing from one step and appearing on the next step instantly, without moving across the space in between. On the quantum staircase, the ball can only have certain amounts of energy, corresponding to the energy of each step, or level. It cannot have any in-between energy.

Balls on staircases don't behave like this. They bounce down, moving through space from one step to another. But electrons in atoms don't pass through any in-between states; they really do make quantum leaps.

Atoms are made up of a tiny central **nucleus** surrounded by a cloud of **electrons**. The nucleus has positive electric charge and the electrons have negative electric charge, so the energy of each electron depends on its position in the atom. The energy levels that the electrons can sit on are like steps on an uneven staircase. An electron can jump from one step to another in a quantum leap, but it cannot be anywhere in between. When an electron jumps down an energy level, the atom radiates a burst of light called a **photon**. If a photon with

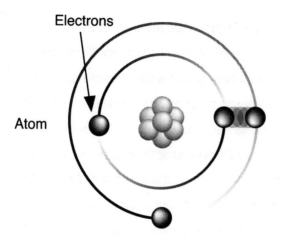

Electrons

Atom

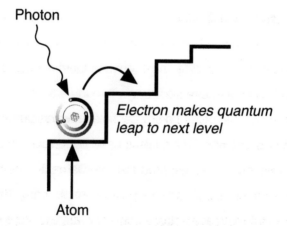

Photon

Electron makes quantum leap to next level

Atom

the right amount of energy hits the atom, an electron can jump up to a higher energy level. And that's quantum leaping.

Scientists know all this from studying the way light is radiated and absorbed by atoms. They began to understand what is going on in the first decades of the twentieth century, just about the time Einstein was working out his theories of relativity. One of the most puzzling discoveries was that photons behave like little particles of light, or little bullets. Until then, physicists had thought of light as a kind of electromagnetic wave – but how could it be a particle and a wave at the same time? Then, in the 1920s the puzzle got even stranger. They discovered that electrons, which physicists thought of as particles, could also behave like waves! What was going on?

Particles and Waves

In the everyday world, waves and particles seem to be two separate things. The difference between them is obvious if you watch what happens when they go through a small hole. Waves spread out on the other side of the hole, but particles keep on going in a single line. Ripples on a pond bend round corners, and spread out. An expert footballer like David Beckham might be able to make a ball bend round a corner, but they would never be able to make it spread out afterwards like the ripples on a pond.

Light has a very small wavelength, so to see this effect actually working for light you need a very small hole, like a slit cut with a razor blade in a sheet of thin card. If you make two slits like this, parallel to one another, and shine a light through the slits in a dark room, waves spread out from each of the slits, like the ripples made by two pebbles dropped into a still pond at the same time. Just like the ripples on a pond, the ripples of light overlap with one another and make a complicated pattern. If you hold another sheet of plain white card up on the other side of the two slits from the light, this pattern shows up as alternating stripes of bright light and darkness, called an **interference pattern**. This proves that light moves like a wave.

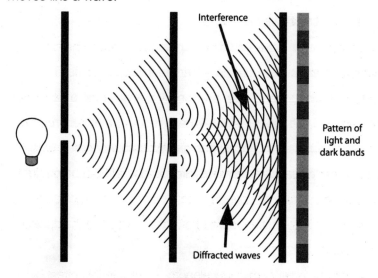

Interference

Pattern of light and dark bands

Diffracted waves

If you had a wall with two holes in it, and you kicked a lot of footballs through the holes, they would not form an interference pattern. They would just pile up in two heaps, one behind each hole. You would be amazed if you found that the balls ended up in a row of neat little piles with empty space between them. Physicists were just as amazed in the 1920s, when they did the same kind of experiments with electrons, and found that they made interference patterns. This proves that electrons travel like waves.

But other experiments also showed that when photons or electrons actually hit atoms they behave like particles. They arrive there with a solid thump, instead of lapping up like waves on the seashore. Modern versions of the experiment with two holes are so sensitive that they can send single photons, or single electrons, through the experiment one at a time. The detectors on the other side are like TV screens where each particle makes a spot of light when it hits and they can measure the arrival of each individual particle. When hundreds or thousands of particles are sent through one after another, the

pattern they build up on the detectors on the other side is an interference pattern.

It's as if each particle spreads out into a wave, goes through both holes in the experiment at once, then collapses back into being a particle when it is measured on the detectors. This is called the collapse of the wave function. In the quantum world, things like electrons and photons are some kind of combination of wave and particle. This is known as *wave-particle duality*.

Nobody understands how this can happen. Richard Feynman, one of the greatest scientists who ever lived, called it "a mystery". But there is no doubt that it happens. Our everyday ideas about things like waves and particles do not apply to things like atoms, light and electrons, just as our everyday ideas about space and time do not apply to things moving near the speed of light, or in strong gravitational fields. All we can do is work out the implications of what the experiments tell us. And one implication is that the world is a very uncertain place – the future is not predetermined.

The Certainty of Uncertainty

Since everything in the world is made up of atoms, everything is a mixture of particle and wave – but we don't see wave-particle duality in the everyday world because we are too big.

Every object has a wavelength which is related to its mass. The wavelength changes according to the way the object moves, that is, its velocity, and mass times velocity is called **momentum**; so, strictly speaking, the wavelength is related to the momentum. For any object, wavelength multiplied by momentum is equal to a constant number, called **Planck's constant**. This is usually written down as the letter h.

In other words, the wavelength of an object – a football, or an electron, or an Olympic 100-metres runner – is equal to h divided by its momentum. Even light has momentum, because it carries energy. The same rules apply to light, but it is easier to get a grip on them by looking at electrons.

Planck's constant is absolutely tiny. In units where we measure mass in grams, it is equal to a decimal point followed by 26 zeroes and two sixes. So the wavelength of an object is too small to measure, let alone notice, unless its momentum is also very small. In practice, this means the mass has to be small. In the same units, the mass of an electron is given by a decimal point followed by 27 zeroes and a 9, which is the same sort of size as h. So the quantum rules only directly affect small things. But that doesn't mean they are not important to us.

The way electrons work is important for microwave ovens, computer chips, lasers like the ones in DVD players, and many more things that we take for granted in everyday life. They are also important in linking atoms together to make molecules, including the molecule of life, DNA. All of these things work on quantum principles, including wave-particle duality. When the quantum rules are applied to atomic nuclei, among other things they explain how the Sun stays hot. If the quantum rules were different, we literally would not be here.

Like relativity theory, quantum theory has passed every test we can think of. There is no doubt that it really does describe how the world works. And one of the most important things it describes is *uncertainty*, which is closely related to wave-particle duality.

The importance of uncertainty in the quantum world was worked out by Werner Heisenberg, a German scientist, in 1927. So it is often called Heisenberg's Uncertainty Principle. But it isn't something he invented – it is part of the way the world really works.

Heisenberg discovered that in the quantum world it is impossible for anything except things like the speed of light, c, and Planck's constant, h, to have precise values. There is always uncertainty. And he found that uncertainty always involves pairs of properties, called conjugate variables. The simplest example of that is the uncertainty in the position of an object compared with the uncertainty in its momentum. The uncertainty in position multiplied by the uncertainty in momentum is always bigger than Planck's constant. Momentum involves velocity, and velocity involves both speed and direction. So uncertainty in momentum means uncertainty in either speed, or direction, or both.

In other words, the more accurately you know where the object is, the less accurately you know where it is going; and the more accurately you know where it is going, the less accurately you know where it is.

This is easy to understand in terms of wave-particle duality, which shows why Planck's constant comes in – it's Planck's constant that links the wave and particle natures of a quantum object. A wave is a spread out thing. You can't have a wave that exists simply at a point. But a wave is always going somewhere. A pure particle could exist at a point, but it would not have any direction at the point. To have a direction, it would have to be moving between two points.

The more a quantum object such as an electron behaves like a wave, the less it behaves like a particle, and the other way round. If it has a definite wavelength, its position is very uncertain; if it has a definite position, its wavelength is very uncertain.

This isn't anything to do with the difficulty for us human beings of measuring the exact position and momentum of something as small as an electron. The electron itself cannot "know" both exactly where it is and exactly where it is going. Depending on what the electron is doing, such as going through the experiment with two holes, or arriving at a detector screen, either one of these properties might be pinned down within the limits set by Planck's constant, but only by "forgetting" the other one.

This changes what scientists think about singularities. In fact, it means that singularities cannot exist. A singularity would be a mathematical point, with no size in any direction, or perhaps a mathematical line, extending in one dimension but with absolutely no thickness. But Heisenberg's Uncertainty Principle tells us that it is impossible for anything to have a precise position, so such a thing cannot exist. The equations actually tell us that there is a smallest possible size for anything, the quantum of size. It is called the **Planck length**, because once again Planck's constant comes into it. Admittedly, the Planck length is very small – in centimetres, roughly a decimal point followed by 32 zeroes and a 1, which is about one hundredth of a billionth of a billionth the size of a **proton**. But the important point is that it is *not* zero. Quantum physics tells us that the general theory of relativity is not the whole story when it comes to understanding what goes on inside black holes, and as we shall see, that opens the way for time travel. Quantum physics also opens the way to an uncertain future.

The Future of Uncertainty

When two billiard balls collide and bounce off each other, it is possible to predict, from the laws of physics, exactly where they will go after the collision. There is no uncertainty about their future. If things like atoms and electrons behaved like that, there would be nothing uncertain about our future. Every collision between particles since the beginning of the Universe would follow the same laws as colliding billiard balls. The entire future of the Universe would be set up in advance by the way the particles were moving in the beginning.

This would mean that when we think we are making independent decisions this isn't really the case. Even the electrons in our brains would be following the same laws of physics so every decision we made would have been set up at the birth of the Universe. It really would be like the image of a fixed past and future, with our awareness rolling through it like a ride in a theme park, that H. G. Wells described in *The Time Machine*. But because of quantum uncertainty, even the electrons themselves do not "know" exactly how they will move after they have interacted with one another. Nothing is certain until it actually happens and the wave collapses.

Nobody understands how this collapse happens. But the fact that it does means that the future is uncertain – which means that when we make decisions about what to do we really are changing the way the future unfolds. But things like billiard balls are much more predictable. If you could hit a perfect shot, you would get a pot every time with no uncertainty. That's simply because Planck's constant is so small.

If Planck's constant were big enough, things like billiard balls and cars in the everyday world would behave like electrons do,

and experience quantum uncertainty. If they did, it would be literally true that it would be impossible to know both how fast a car was going and where it was. The driver would know either how fast the car was going, or where it was, but not both things together. In the quantum world, one thing that is certain is – uncertainty. And that means that the quantum world is ruled by probability.

Probability Rules

When an electron moves, quantum uncertainty means that there is no way to tell for certain where it will end up. All you can do is work out the probability of it arriving at one place rather than another. In the two slit experiment, the electron itself doesn't "know" whether it has gone through one slit or the other, or through both of them. If you throw a ball through the air, from the moment the ball leaves your hand its path and its landing place are determined by the speed and direction it is thrown. Electrons are not like that. When an electron passes through the experiment with two holes, there is no pre-determined path taking it to a definite spot on the detector screen. But there are rules of probability which say that it is more likely to hit one part of the detector rather than another. It is almost certain to end up in one of the bright stripes. But even then, there is no way to tell in advance which stripe it will turn up in. Even if two electrons are fired one after another in the same direction at the same speed they are unlikely to turn up in the same place on the other side of the slits.

These rules of quantum probability are very precise. If you toss a coin, assuming the coin is properly balanced the chances of getting heads or tails are 50:50. That doesn't mean that every time you get heads the next toss will come up tails; but if you toss the coin a thousand times you will get very close to 500 heads and 500 tails. In the same way, the chances of an electron hitting a particular stripe on the detector screen might be 20 per cent (1 in 5). There is no way to tell which electrons will end up there, but if you fire a thousand electrons through the experiment you would find very close to 200 arriving in that stripe. Each electron seems to "know" about the whole setup of the experiment – the two holes, the detector screen and so on. Because this means that electrons and other quantum entities are influenced by things at a distance from them, it is called non-locality. Don't worry if you find this hard to understand. Quantum physicists find it hard to understand, as well. In fact, Richard Feynman used to say that "nobody understands how quantum physics can be like that."

On this picture, an electron that is not being "observed" in some way does not exist at a definite place at all. If you look for it, there is a particular probability that you will find it in one place, another probability that you will find it in another particular place, and so on. But in principle it could turn up literally anywhere in the Universe. Some places are very likely – the bright stripes in the interference pattern. Some places are very unlikely – the dark parts of the pattern. But it is actually possible, though very unlikely indeed, that the electron fired towards the two slits in an experiment on Earth could turn up somewhere else entirely, such as on the surface of the Moon.

Once the electron is observed, the probabilities change. If the electron is found on the surface of the Moon, at that moment the wave function collapses and you know for sure that it is on the Moon. Then the waves start spreading out again, but only from the place the electron was last seen. So now the most likely place to find the electron will be somewhere nearby on the surface of the Moon. When you locate the electron, the wave collapses, but once you stop looking the wave spreads out from the last place it collapsed. It becomes non-local again.

This highlights one of the strangest things about quantum physics. Imagine a box which contains a single electron. If nobody looks inside the box, the electron wave fills the whole box evenly and there is an equal chance of finding the electron anywhere in the box. Now imagine that a partition slides down into the box, dividing it into two halves. If the electron were a ball, you would know that it must be on one side of the partition or the other. But according to the quantum rules, as long as nobody looks, even after the box is divided into two compartments the wave fills the whole box. There is a 50:50 chance of finding the electron on one side of the partition or the other, but the wave doesn't collapse until you look. At that moment, the wave collapses and the electron is located in one half of the box. Now, when you stop looking the wave spreads out again, but only to fill that half of the box.

This kind of behaviour worried Erwin Schrödinger, one of the quantum pioneers. In 1935 he dreamed up an imaginary puzzle, a "thought experiment", to highlight what this kind of behaviour implies.

The Many Worlds of Schrödinger's Cat

Schrödinger imagined setting up an experiment in which the

probabilities of the quantum world could affect something big enough to see – a cat. [*Before we go any further, we should say that nobody has ever done anything like the experiment we are going to describe to a real cat; it is just an imaginary example to highlight what the equations show.*] The heart of the imaginary experiment is a quantum device that can be balanced in a 50:50 state, like the electron wave in the divided box. Schrödinger actually suggested a different setup involving radioactive atoms, but the principle is the same so we might as well stick with the electron in the box. Everything is done just as we have described, up to the point where the partition is lowered down and the electron wave fills both halves of the box. There is a 50:50 chance that, when someone looks, the electron will be found in one half of the box or the other.

This electron box is imagined to be in a large room, completely sealed off from the outside world. In that room, a cat lives comfortably with an ample supply of food and water. But the electron box is wired up to what Schrödinger called "a diabolical device". This is an automatic switch which flips one way or the other when a detector locates the electron. If the electron is found to be in one half of the box, the diabolical device will flood the room with poison, killing the cat. But if the electron is found in the other half of the box, the device will be de-activated and the cat will live. The detector is set to make the measurement at some particular time, and the door to the room stays shut for an hour after that time.

There is no problem understanding what you would see if you were in the room when the electron is detected. Either the imaginary cat lives or dies. But what happens if there is nobody there to make the observations that make the wave collapse? According to the understanding of the quantum rules in Schrödinger's time, instead of the detector making the electron wave collapse, the uncertainty about the state of the electron spreads out into the detector, which can't tell which half of the box the electron is in. After all, the detector and the device are all made of quantum entities such as electrons and atoms.

The diabolical device becomes poised in a kind of mixed state, with the all-important switch both on and off at the same time. So the poison is both released and not released at the same time.

Everything in the room, including the imaginary cat, is poised in a mixed state. After an hour, the experimenters look in through the door and see either a dead cat or a live

*Schrödinger's dead-
and-alive cat?*

cat. But the wave only collapses at that point. Just before they open the door, according to this idea of collapsing wave functions, everything in the room, including the cat, must be in an indeterminate state. The cat must be both dead and alive at the same time.

If the ideas people had in the 1930s were correct, the room could not contain either a live cat or a dead cat until it was observed. What worried Schrödinger, and a lot of other people, was that the equations that made this bizarre prediction are the same equations that explain the way electrons behave in the experiment with two holes, and all the other experiments ever done, and in all the practical devices that use electricity. It seemed you couldn't have the benefits of quantum physics without almost literally losing your grip on reality.

It took twenty years for someone to come up with a good answer to this puzzle. His name was Hugh Everett, and in the 1950s he was working at Princeton University. Everett took an idea that is often found in science fiction and made it real science. It is the idea that there might be other worlds, existing somehow alongside our own world, where history turned out differently. These are sometimes called **parallel universes**, and the idea is often called the **Many Worlds Hypothesis.**

There are lots of stories that use the idea. What if the South had won the American Civil War? What if the two World Wars had ended differently? But Everett asked, what if every possible result of a quantum experiment actually happened? Take Schrödinger's cat. What if, when the experiment is carried out, the universe splits into two copies of itself? In one reality the cat is dead, and in the other reality it is alive. But there is no reality in which it is dead and alive at the same time. It would mean that there are universes where the South won the Civil War or John Lennon wasn't shot, all existing alongside each other like the pages in a book, with a slightly different version of the same story written on every page.

It's easy to make up stories using ideas like this in science fiction. The idea of parallel worlds even turns up in the second instalment of the *Back to the Future* movie trilogy. But science depends on carrying out experiments to test ideas. What Everett did that was special, fifty years ago, was to prove that the Many Worlds idea exactly matches the results of all the experiments. The collapsing wave function idea does too. There is no way to tell which idea is right. So you can choose which one you like best.

If you don't like the idea of cats being dead and alive at the same time, the Many Worlds idea looks a better bet. The snag is, it says that there must be a huge number of different versions of reality, all as real as each other. For example, every time an electron goes through the experiment with two holes, the universe splits into two copies. In one universe the electron goes through one hole, and in the other universe the electron goes through the other hole. But everything else is just the same in the two universes! Two copies of you, and everyone, and everything around us. If the entire world splits every time an electron has a "choice", it would make a huge number of universes.

But David Deutsch, of the University of Oxford, has a way round this. Picking up where Everett left off, he says that the interference pattern on the other side of the experiment is made when the two electrons from the different realities come back together again and fuse into one. That's how the electron can go through both holes at once – only the bit of the universe involving the experiment splits into two, just for the time the electron is travelling through the experiment. To make a long-lasting alternative reality, you need a much bigger "experiment" involving a much bigger change. The kind of change you might be able to make by travelling in time.

Erwin Schrödinger (1887-1961)

Erwin Schrödinger was born in Vienna on 12 August 1887. He came from an affluent family, and was educated by a tutor until 1898, when he started at the high school in Vienna. He went on to the University of Vienna in 1906, completing his courses in 1910. After a year of compulsory military service he went back to the university as a teacher. During the First World War, he served as an artillery officer, but returned to his job at the university when the war ended. In 1920, Schrödinger got married, and moved to Germany. Over the next few years he worked at universities in Jena, Stuttgart, and Breslau. Then, in 1921 he settled down as a Professor of Physics in Zurich.

It was in Zurich that Schrödinger did his most important work. In 1926 he found an equation that describes how things like electrons behave in the quantum world. This became known as the Schrödinger equation. It was a great breakthrough at the time, nearly as important as the general theory of relativity, and as a result Schrödinger was appointed as Professor of Physics in Berlin.

Most professors in those days, especially in

Germany, were very rigid, formal people who liked rules and regulations. Schrödinger was different. Another great quantum physicist, Paul Dirac, has described how Schrödinger would turn up by train for an important scientific meeting and "walk from the station to the hotel where the delegates stayed, carrying all his luggage in a rucksack and looking so like a tramp that it needed a great deal of argument at the reception desk before he could claim a room." All this helped to make him very popular with the students, and he was an excellent teacher.

Schrödinger was happy in Berlin, but in 1933 Hitler came to power and the Nazis began persecuting the Jews. Although he was not Jewish himself, Schrödinger resigned his job and left Germany in protest. He visited Oxford and Princeton over the next few years, then returned to Austria, his homeland, and took up a post at the University of Graz in 1936.

In spite of all this turmoil, it was in 1935 that Schrödinger dreamed up his famous "cat in a box" experiment, during a debate with his friend Albert Einstein. As he put it, once the experiment has been set up in the way we describe in this chapter, until somebody looks in to the box, it has in it "the living and the dead cat mixed or smeared out in equal parts".

Just two years after Schrödinger started working in Graz, Nazi Germany took over Austria. Schrödinger and his wife escaped to Italy, then moved on to Oxford and Ghent. They were only able to settle down properly again when the Institute for Advanced Studies was set up in Dublin, especially to provide a base for him and to use his fame to give a boost to Irish science. He became the first Director of the School for Theoretical Physics at the Institute, and stayed there until he retired in 1955. He even became an Irish citizen.

In 1944, Schrödinger wrote a little book called What is Life? This dealt with the idea of a genetic code. It was a big influence on many biologists, including James Watson, who, together with Francis Crick, discovered the double-helix structure of DNA.

After he retired from the Dublin job, Schrödinger went back to Vienna where he was given an honorary post at the university in 1956. But he suffered a severe illness in 1957, and had to retire for a second time in 1958. He died of tuberculosis on 4 January 1961.

Chapter 4

Two Ways to Build a Time Machine

Science fiction writer Larry Niven once wrote a story called "Rotating cylinders and the possibility of global causality violation". You can find the story in his collection *Convergent Series*. It's not the kind of title you might expect for a science fiction story, but that's because Niven lifted it, as he acknowledges, from the prestigious scientific journal *Physical Review*. There, it was the title of a serious scientific paper written by the American physicist Frank Tipler. The reason why this scientific paper attracted the attention of a science fiction writer is that expression "causality violation".

We expect things to happen after the effects that cause them. If you flip the light switch by the door, the light goes on just after you flip the switch, not before. That's normal causality. If the light came on before you flipped the switch, the cause would come after the effect – that's causality violation. One explanation for this would be if flipping the switch sent a signal backwards in time to turn the light on before the switch was flipped. It's the kind of explanation you would expect in science fiction, but Tipler showed how it could really happen. And *then* it became part of a science fiction story. Causality violation means some kind of distortion of time, perhaps even time travel. Frank Tipler's serious scientific paper proved that time travel is possible.

The key point is that time travel is not forbidden by the general theory of relativity, which is the same thing as saying that it is possible. Even before Tipler came along and made his calculations, other people had found that Einstein's equations allow for the possibility that a traveller could move in a circuit around spacetime – not just through space – returning to the same place *and* the same time they started from. Obviously, in order to do this you would have to travel backward in time for part of your journey. This kind of path through spacetime is called a **closed timelike line**, or **CTL**. Tipler proved that CTLs are indeed permitted by the general theory. Then he asked, how could you actually go on such a journey in the real universe?

Twisting Time

It's all to do with the way matter distorts spacetime. Before, we described a massive object like the Sun making a dent in spacetime, like the dent made by a bowling ball on a trampoline. But what happens if the massive object is rotating? It wouldn't just spin round in the dent, like a bowling ball spinning on the surface of a trampoline. The spinning mass would try to drag spacetime round with it, as if the rubber surface of the trampoline were sticking to the ball. It's a bit like the way if you dip a spoon into a jar of runny honey and twist the spoon round, the honey gets twisted round with the spoon. This dragging of spacetime by a rotating mass is one of the key predictions of the general

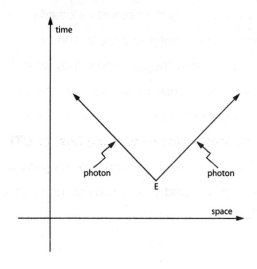

theory of relativity. Although the effect is tiny for the Earth, which is quite small compared with a star and only spins once every 24 hours, it has actually been measured using very sensitive instruments on board satellites orbiting round our planet. There is no doubt that the general theory is right.

Once again, the process involves space and time, not just space. To see how, we need to look at the spacetime diagrams invented by Hermann Minkowski. If we represent time on the vertical axis, measured in seconds, and space on the horizontal, measured in light-seconds (the distance light travels in one second), then the path of all the light

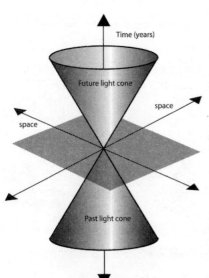

(photons) from a flash of light at event E is at 45 degrees. Since nothing can travel faster than light, the path of any object can never move lower than the 45 degrees line.

If you add a second space dimension to the Minkowski diagram, then the light paths sweep out a cone-shaped funnel. Starting from any point in spacetime, an object, or person, can only move within the cone swept out by the light paths; this is the "light cone". To get anywhere else would involve travelling faster than light – or backwards in time.

The upper-cone (called the future light cone) represents the future history of a light-flash emitted at event E – everywhere the flash goes in space and time after leaving E. The lower-cone (called the past light cone) represents all directions from which light-flashes can be received at event E.

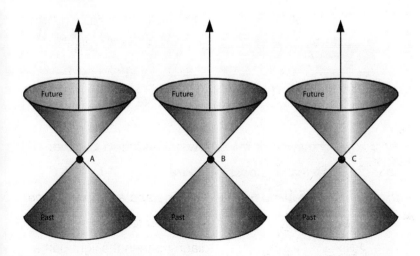

Light cones for spacetime events A, B and C. It is impossible to travel from one of these events to another.

Tipler calculated that the way spacetime is distorted near a very massive, rotating cylinder is equivalent to tipping the light cone over. Close to the spinning cylinder, the light cones are tipped by more than 45 degrees. One of the space dimensions starts acting like time, whilst the time dimension starts acting like space.

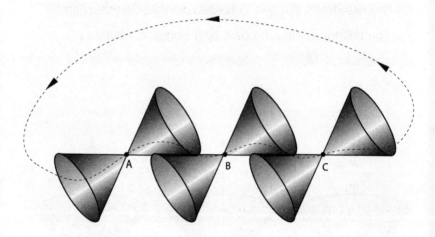

Near a rotating cylinder, the spacetime distortion tips the light cones so that it is possible to travel from A to B to C, then back to the same time and place you started from, without ever travelling faster than light.

From the point of view of someone far away from the rotating cylinder, a spaceship near the spinning mass and travelling into the future as far as its local light cone was concerned would actually be travelling into the past as far as the outside universe was concerned.

It would be possible to steer the spaceship in near the cylinder from the region of flat spacetime, circle round and round the cylinder to go farther and farther back in time, then steer the spaceship back out to the region of flat spacetime, at a point however far back in time you wanted. Then, you could go back in near the cylinder and follow the same process in reverse, heading into the future and the same place and time you started, at the end of a Closed Timelike Line.

It would be very difficult to make a cylinder massive enough and spinning fast enough, to make time travel possible. But the biggest surprise in Tipler's work is that we already know of natural objects in the universe which are on the edge of being time machines. He calculated that in order to make CTLs you would need a cylinder containing at least as much mass as our Sun, about 100 km long and about 10 km wide, spinning twice every millisecond – two thousand times a second. That is very extreme compared with anything on Earth, but not compared with a **pulsar**.

A pulsar is a roughly spherical neutron star containing about twice as much mass as our Sun in a ball about 10 km across. Amazingly, the fastest pulsars known spin nearly a thousand times a second – with only a little exaggeration, they are called "millisecond pulsars". The very fastest pulsar known, discovered in 2006, spins 716 times a second, or once every 1.4 milliseconds, so its equator is moving at a quarter of the speed of light. A Tipler time machine would only have to be spinning three times faster than this.

The biggest problem is stretching the cylinder out long enough. It would be like ten millisecond pulsars joined pole to pole in a chain. You might imagine that a sufficiently advanced spacefaring civilization would be able to move pulsars around and link them together like this. But if you tried this then gravity would make the string of pulsars collapse down along their length, forming a single ball containing twenty or so solar masses of material and disappearing into a black hole. The spacefarers would need some kind of antigravity, to stop the collapse happening.

That isn't a totally mad idea – and it also comes into the story of the second kind of time machine. This time, instead of science being the inspiration for a science fiction story, science fiction was the inspiration for the scientists who worked out how to build a time machine.

Making Contact

This started when the astronomer Carl Sagan decided to write a science fiction story, which became the novel, and then the movie, *Contact*. Sagan wanted a way for his character Eleanor Arroway to travel between the stars – in particular, from our Solar System to the region of the star Vega, just over 25 light years away. As a good scientist, he knew that nothing could travel faster than light, and even light takes more than 25 years to make this journey. But he liked the idea used in many science fiction stories of taking a shortcut through "hyperspace" to get to the destination quicker.

In those stories, the science is usually ignored. The characters in their spaceship dive in to one end of a tunnel through space, sometimes called a wormhole, and pop out somewhere else. But Sagan was a well-known scientist, and didn't want his readers to feel cheated – he wanted the science in his story to be as accurate as possible. So he asked a friend who was an expert on the general theory of relativity, Kip Thorne, for the latest ideas about Einstein-

Rosen bridges and the like.

Until Sagan set them thinking, the relativists had thought that these bridges, or wormholes, could not be real. They thought that even if such wormholes ever opened up, they would collapse again before anyone could travel through them, unless the travellers went faster than light. Even Einstein thought that. But Thorne and his colleagues at the California Institute of Technology (Caltech) found that this was wrong. They found that the known laws of physics allow wormholes to be open for long enough for people to travel through them, although the technology needed for this is way beyond anything we can do today.

Once again, the key is antigravity – or negative energy, which amounts to the same thing. To keep the wormhole open, the walls of the tunnel have to be lined with negative energy material. This produces a gravity force which pushes outwards, and stops the wormhole collapsing. Physicists call this negative energy material "exotic" material. The surprise is that exotic material isn't just allowed for in theory by the equations; there are actually experiments which prove that negative energy exists.

Negative energy exists because of quantum uncertainty. There is always some uncertainty about how much energy there is in any tiny volume of space at any moment in time – if there were exactly zero energy it would be certain. So the quantum rules allow waves and their associated particles to pop into existence for a brief moment, then disappear again – in a sense, before the universe notices they are there. But they are immediately replaced by other temporary particles. "Empty" space is actually a seething broth of these so-called "virtual particles". But by definition, the average energy density of empty space is zero. As long ago as 1948, a Dutch physicist called Hendrik Casimir showed how this can make negative energy.

In empty space, particles (in particular, photons, the particles corresponding to electromagnetic waves) with all kinds of wavelengths can pop into temporary existence in this way. But if you put two metal plates very close together, only particles with the right wavelengths can fit in to the gap between the two plates. This is because the ends of the waves have to be anchored to the plates.

It's the same as the way you can only play certain notes on a guitar string, because the ends of the string are fixed. That means that there can't be as many waves between the two plates as in the space outside. So there must be, on average, *less* energy between the plates than in the empty space outside. The energy of that empty space outside is zero, so the energy between the plates is less than zero – it is negative. As a result, the extra energy outside pushes the two plates together.

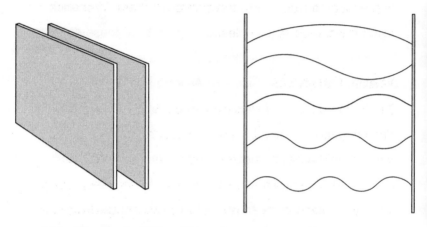

This "**Casimir Effect**" has been measured in experiments. It is very small, but it is real. Negative energy exists. So one way to keep the mouths of a wormhole open would be to line them with pairs of large metal plates, providing the negative energy needed so that the wormhole's higher energy pushes against them.

There are also other ways in which it might be possible, in theory, to make negative energy. The important thing about the Casimir Effect is that it has been measured and it exists, so we know negative energy is real. It would be very, very difficult to build a wormhole, but physicists such as Kip Thorne aren't too worried about that. They are happy to leave those problems to the engineers of the future. What matters is that the laws of physics allow wormholes to exist long enough for people to travel through them. These are called traversable wormholes.

Time Tunnels

Carl Sagan used these ideas in his story to explain how Eleanor Arroway could travel to Vega and back through a wormhole. The physicists at Caltech were delighted, and went on to work out how exotic matter would affect things like black holes. At first, they were so preoccupied with this that they forgot that a wormhole is a tunnel through spacetime, not just a tunnel through space. Then, a physicist called Tom Roman pointed out that if you can use a wormhole for space travel, you can also use it for time travel.

This set the Caltech team thinking about time travel, and eventually they published their recipe for building a time machine in the journal *Physical Review Letters*. That set other physicists thinking about time travel, and for the past twenty years scientists have taken the idea of time travel seriously and published scientific papers and books about time travel and time machines. All thanks to the inspiration of Carl Sagan and his science fiction story that doesn't even involve time travel!

Kip Thorne himself has described the simplest way to turn a wormhole into a time machine, in his book *Black Holes and Time Warps*.

It all depends on the **twin effect**. Suppose you have a wormhole a few metres long, with one end in a laboratory on Earth and the other in a spaceship sitting on the ground outside the lab. If the wormhole is big enough, you could get from the lab to the spaceship instantly by crawling through it. When you did so, your head and arms might be in the spaceship while your feet and legs were still in the lab, but you wouldn't feel anything odd. The time in the spaceship would be the same as the time in the lab, and it would take no time at all to go through the wormhole from one place to the other.

Now, go back to the lab while your twin sister sets off on a journey in the spaceship at very high speed, taking her end of the wormhole with her. Kip Thorne imagines a journey that lasts for 12 hours according to the clock in the spaceship – six hours there and six back – but lasts for ten years according to the clocks in the lab. When your sister returns, she will be ten years younger than you – and her end of the wormhole will be ten years "younger" than the end in the lab. If she crawls through the wormhole from the spaceship back into the lab, she will arrive ten years earlier, on the day she was setting out on her journey. But if someone in the lab crawled through the wormhole they would emerge in the spaceship ten years in the future.

As long as nobody moved the spaceship again, you could do this as often as you like. Crawl through the wormhole ten years into the future, then walk back to the lab, crawl through the hole again another ten years into the future, and so on. Once you had visited the future you could get back to your own time by crawling through the hole in the spaceship to get back to the lab, then walking out to the spaceship and crawling through the hole again, and so on.

For now, we won't go into the paradoxes that might arise if a time tunnel existed – what would happen, for example, if your sister crawled through the wormhole from the spaceship back into the lab ten years earlier, then walked out to the spaceship and met her younger self? Kip Thorne discovered an important fact, which applies to all time machines. In every case, it is impossible to go back farther in

time than the moment when the time machine was created. You can go back to the time that the spaceship took off, but no farther, *because the time machine did not exist before then*.

It turns out that this is a law of physics that applies to all time machines. For example, if exotic matter really exists, it could be used to stop a Tipler time machine collapsing into a black hole, and spaceships really would be able to go back in time by orbiting round such a spinning cylinder in the right way. But they could never go back in time before the spinning cylinder was created.

Why is this so important? Because the main reason people who don't believe in time travel object to the idea is that there are no time travellers around today. If time travel is possible, why aren't we overrun with tourists from the future? Simple – because the time machine hasn't *yet* been invented. As soon as it is, there will probably be crowds from the future jumping out of it to greet us, even before we get a chance to test it. That won't happen for a long time yet, because if Kip Thorne is right we'll need to make a traversable wormhole first, and that isn't going to be easy.

Building a Time Machine

Perhaps in the future space travellers might find a natural wormhole in spacetime that they can use as a time machine. Failing that, the best bet seems to be to take advantage of quantum effects to make a tiny wormhole, then turn it into a time machine. Even if it wasn't big enough for people to go through, a small time tunnel that we could look through, into the past or the future, would be a dramatic achievement.

It might be done by starting out with the foamy fabric of spacetime at the Planck length (see page 74). Nobody knows for sure what happens at such tiny distances. According to experts like Kip Thorne, the best bet is that spacetime itself is made of a kind of foamy structure, like the froth on a breaking wave on the seashore, with a mixture of all kinds of loops, bridges, tunnels and wormholes bubbling away in what is known as the "quantum foam". These different kinds of temporary spacetime structures are allowed by quantum uncertainty; they are equivalent to the virtual particles that pop in and out of existence all the time in "empty space" on a larger scale. Quantum foam is everywhere – in Thorne's words, "inside black holes, in interstellar space, in the room where you sit, in your brain." It is what the world is made of. It makes the structure of spacetime, like the threads in carpet making up the fabric of the carpet; but it would be a very weird carpet, with the threads constantly changing their colour and thickness; even what they are made of and their position in the carpet.

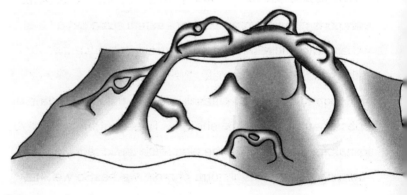

Quantum foam

Even this idea has made it into science fiction. In Philip Pullman's *His Dark Materials* trilogy, one of the main characters, Will, comes into possession of a knife so sharp that it can unpick the threads of spacetime itself; with it, he can cut holes, rather like wormholes, through into other worlds. Physicists like Thorne think that this really might be possible, although it would need more than a very sharp knife to do it.

They think that quantum foam also contains virtual wormholes, which exist for a tiny fraction of a second before disappearing again. These could be turned into real, long-lasting wormholes simply by giving them enough energy. The same kind of thing can be done with virtual photons – in fact, we do it all the time in TV and radio transmitters. An electric field is made of a cloud of virtual photons popping in and out of existence around a charged particle such as an electron. When we give the electrons energy and make them move along a wire or through the transmitter aerial, some of the energy gets absorbed by the virtual photons. These get turned into real photons that make up the electromagnetic radiation moving outward in the form of radio waves. So we know the trick works.

It would need an even greater amount of energy to turn a virtual wormhole into a real wormhole, but as always physicists leave the details to future generations of engineers. It's not so much the total amount of energy you need that's the problem, but concentrating the energy in one very small bubble. Today, particle physicists concentrate energy almost at a point by colliding beams of fast-moving particles – things like protons, or even atomic nuclei – using giant accelerators like the one at **CERN**, near Geneva. In the future, even bigger accelerators might be built on the Moon, or in space. There is no technical reason why they couldn't concentrate enough energy in a tiny bubble for it to make a virtual wormhole real.

Once you've got a tiny wormhole, the next step is to inflate it. Remember scientists will only be able to make a time machine if they have exotic matter (negative energy pushing outwards against gravity) to hold the wormhole open, so that has to be taken for granted as part of the process. Exotic material is also just what you need to inflate a wormhole. If it is threaded through the wormhole, the antigravity effect will open up the hole nicely. It doesn't need to be big enough to be traversable, just big enough to manipulate.

With Kip Thorne's imaginary traversable wormhole, one end of the hole had to be taken on a journey into space to turn it into a time machine. But if we had a tiny wormhole, it would be possible to do the same thing much more easily. First, you'd have to squirt electrons into it to make it electrically charged, so that you could get hold of the ends of the wormhole using electric and magnetic fields and move them around. Then, you'd need to put one end into a circular particle accelerator, where it would whizz round at nearly the speed of light to build up a time difference between the two ends. This is exactly the way the twin effect has actually been measured for radioactive particles, so we know it would work. The only snag is that to build up a time difference of ten years you would need to run the machine for ten years; to make a time tunnel a hundred years long you'd have to wait for a hundred years; and so on. But surely, it would be worth the wait!

You'd be left with a narrow time tunnel that could be used to send particles forward or back in time, or that you could peep through, using a microscope, for a look into the past or the future. Then, if you wanted a traversable wormhole – a human-sized time machine – you'd have to expand it some more using exotic material.

That wouldn't be easy. But what matters is that it would be possible, according to the laws of physics and everything we know about the Universe. Leonardo Da Vinci, who lived from 1452 to 1519, couldn't build an aeroplane. But he knew that flying machines were possible. More than five hundred years ago he drew designs for aircraft that could be built today and would actually fly if they were powered by modern engines. In five hundred years from now, in the 26th century, engineers might very well have the kind of engines needed to inflate wormholes out of the quantum foam and turn them into time machines, using exactly the kind of blueprints sketched out by Kip Thorne and his colleagues.

Black Holes and Baby Universes

If the engineers of the future really are able to manipulate wormholes, they may not use them only for travelling between the stars in our Universe, like Eleanor Arroway, or as time machines, like the characters in TV's *Time Tunnel*. There is another possibility, which has been highlighted by the work of several scientists, including Stephen Hawking, of the University of Cambridge. This is the idea of "baby universes".

What happens to anything that falls into a black hole? According to the general theory of relativity, it has to literally disappear in the singularity inside the black hole. But quantum theory has shown us that the singularity cannot actually exist, and what lies at the heart of the hole must be an extreme version of the quantum foam, at the **Planck scale**.

The only alternative to describing singularities in terms of the general theory of relativity is to describe them in terms of quantum theory. This means inventing a quantum theory of gravity, and nobody has yet done this properly, because it is so difficult. One way to try to do it is to use wave functions, like the waves that are associated with things like electrons. Hawking has tried to work out what a wave function for the entire universe would look like. Even he can't write down the equation for the actual wave function for the entire universe, but he thinks he can say what it would be like. The most important discovery is that like the wave functions in Schrödinger's imaginary "cat in the box" experiment, all the possible waves would exist at the same time. Stephen Hawking believes that this means that all possible universes exist at the same time. That might explain what happens to everything that falls into a black hole – it gets shunted through another kind of wormhole into another universe.

Some of these ideas have been developed by Lee Smolin, a physicist based in New York. If scientists like Hawking and Smolin are right, it means that our entire universe, everything that astronomers can ever see with their telescopes, is not everything that there is. It would mean that our universe is just one bubble among very many universes, perhaps an infinite number of universes. The bubbles would be connected to one another by tiny wormholes, far too small to travel through.

This is called the "baby universes" idea because although a black hole in one universe would make a tiny wormhole in spacetime, the other end of the wormhole might inflate naturally to make a new universe. This is not a completely crazy idea. All the evidence astronomers have gathered from their observations of our universe fits in with the idea that the universe we can see started very small indeed, much smaller than an atom, but got inflated by the outward pressure of a kind of antigravity, which only lasted for a short time. This idea is known as cosmic inflation, and it is exactly the same, but involving much more energy, as the kind of inflation that an advanced civilization could use

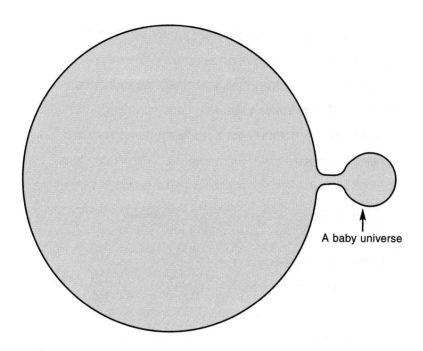

A baby universe

to expand tiny wormholes up to a traversable size.

Natural inflation seems to be what got our universe started. If it could get our universe started, it could do the same thing for other universes. Just as our universe could make "babies" in this way, our universe itself might be the "baby" produced by a black hole that collapsed in another universe. If our descendants five hundred years from now really do have engines capable of expanding quantum wormholes up to traversable size, they might be able to use them to open gateways to other universes.

It's a fascinating idea, although it may seem to be wandering from the theme of time travel; but maybe it isn't such a detour after all. Physicists could get round the problems of paradoxes caused by time travel, and that takes us right back to Schrödinger's cat, wave functions, and parallel universes.

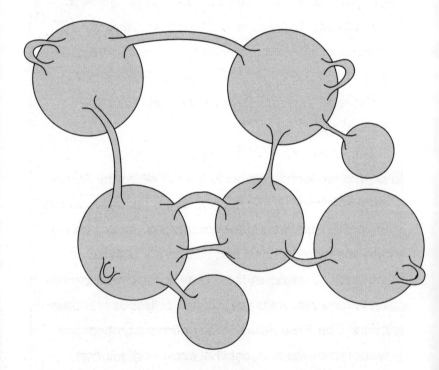

Connected universes – each a spacetime bubble

Carl Sagan (1934-1996)

Carl Sagan was born in Brooklyn, New York, on 9 November 1934. He graduated from Rahway High School in 1951. He then studied at the University of Chicago, receiving his first degree in 1955, a Master's degree in 1956, and a doctorate in astronomy and astrophysics in 1960. He worked at the Smithsonian Astrophysical Laboratory and taught at Harvard University until 1968, when he moved to Cornell University. He became a Professor at Cornell in 1971, and was the Director of their Laboratory for Planetary Studies.

Sagan was involved in the American space programme from its early days, and briefed the Apollo astronauts on scientific aspects of their missions to the Moon. He contributed ideas to many of the unmanned missions to the planets, and was responsible for attaching messages to the Pioneer and Voyager probes just in case they might be picked up by aliens. In Star Trek V: The Final Frontier, one of these probes is destroyed by the Klingons. He was one of the first people to realise that the surface of Venus must be a hot, dry desert because of the greenhouse effect of its thick atmosphere, and he encouraged Jim Lovelock to develop Gaia theory, the idea that both living and non-living systems on planet Earth are part of a single system that maintains conditions suitable for life.

Sagan was fascinated by the possibility that other

intelligent life forms might exist in the universe, and promoted the idea of the search for extraterrestrial intelligence (SETI) using radio telescopes to listen out for signals from space. He worked with the astronomer Frank Drake on a radio message beamed out into space from the Arecibo telescope in Puerto Rico on 16 November 1974. So far, there hasn't been an answer.

One of Sagan's more practical concerns was the danger that a large comet or asteroid might hit the Earth, causing devastation on the scale of the impact that killed off the dinosaurs 65 million years ago. He urged governments to set up a search for such objects, in the hope that if one is discovered approaching the Earth it might be deflected before it can do any harm.

Alongside all his scientific work, Sagan was an enthusiastic populariser of science. He made a very successful TV series, Cosmos, and wrote a book to go with the series, as well as other popular science books. The novel Contact, which accidentally set Kip Thorne and his colleagues thinking about time travel, was published in 1985. Sagan was not a great scientist himself, although he was a very good one, but by his enthusiasm and his encouragement of other people he made a very important contribution to science. He also made a point of debunking pseudoscience, such as astrology and belief in UFOs, with carefully worked out, detailed arguments.

Sagan married three times and had five children.

One of those children, Nick Sagan, became a writer, and contributed several episodes in the various later series of Star Trek spinoffs.

Carl Sagan died on 20 December 1996, in Seattle, Washington, after a long fight with the illness myelodysplasia, a cancer affecting the bone marrow.

He once said that "the significance of finding that there are other beings who share this universe with us would be absolutely phenomenal, it would be an epochal event in human history."

Chapter 5

Doctoring the Paradoxes

The most famous time travel paradox is the "Granny paradox". Like the cat in the box "experiment", this is a purely imaginary scenario – no real grannies were harmed. The idea is that a time traveller might go back in time, and accidentally (or even deliberately) kill his own grandmother, his mother's mother, before his mother was even born. In that case, his mother couldn't have been born, so the time traveller wasn't born, so Granny didn't die. In which case, he *was* born, and she *did* die!

Something similar happens in the first of the *Back to the Future* movies, when Marty travels back in time and for a while it looks as if he is going to stop his own parents ever getting married. In the movie, he starts to fade away, but his parents do get together after all and everything is OK. Or is it that simple? If you follow the story closely, you'll see that

Marty's parents *only* get together because he goes back in time – they never would have married if he hadn't interfered with their lives. So Marty is only born because he went back in time to help his parents get together. It's another kind of paradox, a time loop in which the future interferes with the past to make the future that influences the past.

Making History

Naturally, such puzzles have intrigued science fiction writers, who have investigated the implications in many stories. They take delight in finding ways round the puzzles, using the idea that, in a phrase coined by the writer Robert Heinlein, "a Paradox may be Paradoctored". In one of his stories, called *By His Bootstraps* and published as long ago as 1941, Heinlein's young hero accidentally stumbles into the future through a time gate operated by a mysterious old man, who promptly disappears. The young man learns how to operate the time gate, and has many adventures before one day he accidentally scoops up his own younger self. He has become the old man from the start of the story, and moves on to leave his younger self to his new life.

This is one way round the paradoxes – the idea, going right back to H. G. Wells and *The Time Machine*, that all the past and all the future already exists, so that all the adventures of the time traveller are laid out like a ride through a theme park, and there is actually no way to change anything. This "doctors" the Granny paradox by saying that if you did travel back in time, nothing you could do would cause the premature death of your grandmother, because we already know she didn't suffer an untimely death. According to this way of looking at things, there never was a version of the past without you, the time traveller, in it. Whatever you try to do, you must have already done it, because you must have been in the past all along. If you tried to shoot Granny, the gun wouldn't go off; if you put poison in her tea, she wouldn't drink it, and so on.

Several classic science fiction stories use this idea. In Michael Moorcock's story *Behold the Man*, a time traveller goes back to the time of Jesus Christ in the hope of meeting the Messiah. He is baffled to find no trace of the Jesus he knows about from the Bible; but as he goes around asking people for news about the Messiah, from the stories he tells he is taken to be the Messiah himself, and ends up living out Jesus' life, right up to the death on the cross. The message of such stories is that you can't change history, so there are no paradoxes, but you can be part of history, whether you like it or not.

This resolution of the paradoxes won't work, because of quantum effects. In part, this is due to quantum uncertainty. Nothing can be fixed in a definite pattern, not even the past. But it is also because of the different versions of reality allowed by quantum physics. So quantum physics also gives a different perspective on another idea, that goes back to the 1960s.

The idea is that past and future are laid out in time the way the continents are laid out on the surface of the Earth, so that a date like 1st October 1966 is a place in time just as the Golden Gate Bridge in San Francisco is a place in space. This was something that one eminent scientist who also wrote science fiction, Fred Hoyle, took very seriously. He described his version of the idea in a book called *October the First is Too Late*. The book is fiction. It describes a strange disruption of spacetime in which different geographical regions of the Earth seem to be living in different times, from the past and the future, alongside one another. Fred Hoyle based this story on real science.

Fred Hoyle's Universe

Hoyle said that our image of time as an ever-rolling stream is "a grotesque and absurd illusion". He said that everything that was and everything that ever will be already exists – it's as if each moment of time has been put into one of the "pigeon holes" in an array of little shelves like the pigeon holes in an old-fashioned postal sorting office. Hoyle imagined that all the pigeon holes might be arranged in some order, as if they were numbered, and each pigeon hole contains information, like a written history, about all the holes with lower numbers, but not about the holes with higher numbers.

If some kind of superbeing (Hoyle called him "the cosmic postman") came along and looked in one of the holes, he would see there all the information from all the holes lower down the sequence, too: that moment in time and all the moments before it – he would "remember the past". But the postman can look in any hole in any order, jumping about from higher numbers to lower numbers and back again, and wherever he looks he will find information about the past but not about the future.

If Hoyle's imagined model is right, there is no way to change the past. But what if there is more than one set of pigeon holes? And what if "new" stacks of pigeon holes can be made, to provide alternative futures? We are back to Schrödinger's Cat and multiple realities.

In Schrödinger's cat-in-the-box experiment there is an equal chance of the cat being dead or alive, like the equal chance of a tossed coin coming down heads or tails. We don't get into the possible complications of the imaginary cat maybe being two-thirds dead and one-third alive, or nine-tenths dead and one tenth alive. But in real quantum experiments the choices are seldom evenly balanced. Some things are very likely – in the experiment with two holes, it is very likely that any single electron will indeed go through the holes, even if the way it does that is still a mystery. It is very unlikely that the electron will end up on the Moon. Somehow, we have to include all these probabilities if we want to understand how the quantum world works, and how that affects things like cats and people in the everyday world.

The Universe Tree

It is best to start with Hugh Everett's idea, and to take in with it all the quantum probabilities. You can do this if you think of the world as like a tree with many branches – the universe tree. The branches divide into smaller branches, there are twigs growing out of branches, and so on. Thick branches correspond to things that are very likely, and thin branches correspond to things that are less likely. But unlike your typical tree in the woods, any particular branch may get fatter or thinner as it stretches outward away from its neighbours, according to how the probabilities change.

If you pick out a piece of the tree at random, you are more likely to choose a bit of a thick branch than a bit of a slender twig. That corresponds to the probabilities of different results from an experiment like shooting electrons at a screen with two holes.

In the case of Schrödinger's Cat, because there is an

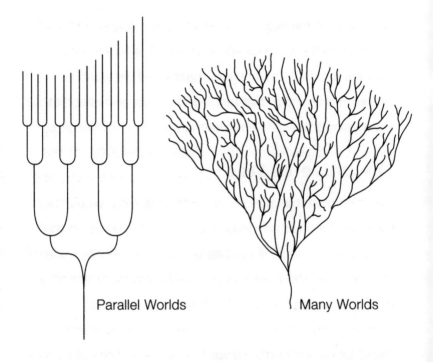

Parallel Worlds   Many Worlds

exact 50:50 chance of the cat being dead or being alive, that means that at the place in the tree (the place in spacetime) corresponding to the experiment one branch of the universe tree forks into two equal-sized branches. In one branch, the cat is alive; in the other branch, it is dead. But the real world is more complicated.

When we toss a coin, we usually say there is a 50:50 chance of it coming down heads or coming down tails. That would correspond to the chance of being in either one of two equal branches after the splitting of a single branch of the universe tree. We usually ignore the tiny chance of the coin landing on its edge and staying balanced upright while it rolls across the floor. But that could happen. It would correspond to a tiny twiglet, branching out from the same fork in the universe tree. And because probabilities always add up exactly to 1 (after all, *something* must happen!), the two main branches stretching out from the fork would each have to be a tiny bit thinner to allow for the "wood" in the twiglet. The chance of getting a head is still the same as the chance of getting a tail, but now each of those probabilities is not 0.5 exactly, but 0.499999999999 …

Every possible result of everything that could ever happen would be represented by a branch or twig of the right size, somewhere in the universe tree. And the whole tree exists "all the time", like Hoyle's cosmic pigeonholes, while our awareness moves along the branches. It isn't that the universe divides into two or more copies whenever there are two or more possibilities. It's just that in one branch there is a stack of pigeon holes with, for example, historical records describing a dead cat, and in the branch next door there is a stack of pigeonholes with historical records describing a live cat. The cosmic postman can look anywhere, on either branch, and he will always find "memories" of a logical, consistent history. Our decisions don't so much create the future as determine which version of the future we move into. But they are still real choices that affect our personal lives.

A Choice of Futures

This gives us a different view of the granny paradox, and of the way science fiction writers have tried to doctor it. If you really did go back in time and try to kill granny, according to the Many Worlds idea you might very well succeed. If you did, you wouldn't suddenly be snuffed out of existence yourself, because you would now (whatever "now" means) be in a different branch of the universe tree. You could travel back to the future up that branch of the tree, and arrive at the time you set out from, only to find that you had never existed in that branch before and nobody knew who you were. At the same time but in your original branch of the tree, your granny and your mother would have led their lives unaware of any of this, but you would have disappeared in your time machine, never to return. It is as if you were born in London then moved to New York; the fact that you had not been born in New York wouldn't mean that you weren't still alive.

In the same way, in *Back to the Future*, if Marty did stop his parents from getting together he would not fade away. He'd just be stuck in a different branch of the tree from where he started.[1] Unless he went even farther back in time and then somehow steered his way forward again into his original branch.

In one episode of *The Simpsons* something like this happens to Homer. He keeps going back in time, changing the past, and coming "home" to one different future after another. But he is not changing "the" future or "the" present (or even the past); he is moving up and down different branches of the universe tree. The cartoon makes the point by exaggerating the kind of things that might happen, but for a real time traveller it would probably be much less obvious that he or she was in a different branch of the universe tree.

Even if you might think you had stayed out of trouble in your own branch of the universe tree, and had been very careful not to do anything drastic like killing your granny when you were in the past, you would never be able to return to *exactly* the place in spacetime you started from.

1 Something like this happens in *Back to the Future II*, when Marty travels "back" to a different future.

The American physicist Jack Sarfatti, who uses the word "universe" where we say "branches", explains what would happen:

We avoid the known paradoxes of time travel because of the many possible universes. A time traveller will probably return to a universe that is different from, but very similar to, the universe from which he started. These different universes usually differ in very subtle ways so that unless the time traveller is very observant he may not even realise he has returned to a different universe.[2]

One thing Sarfatti doesn't look into is the possibility that the time traveller might return to his or her own time, but in a different branch of the universe tree, to find another version of him or her self already there. This is an idea that has been explored in several science fiction stories. It's a paradox that can be doctored away by the same rules of quantum physics that make light travel in straight lines. But first we want to clear up a common misunderstanding about the universe tree, a trap that lots of science fiction writers tumble into.

2 This comes from a book called *Space-Time and Beyond*, by Bob Toben, Dutton, New York, 1974.

Out of the Trap

The trap is the idea that the decisions we take *make* the different versions of the future become real. One of the characters in Fred Hoyle's *October the First Is Too Late* wonders what would happen if a kind of glorified Schrödinger's Cat experiment, a Doomsday Device, was rigged up so that there would be a certain probability of the entire world being destroyed, and some other probability that it would survive:

My guess is that inevitably we appear to survive, because there is a division, the world divides into two, into two completely disparate stacks of pigeon holes. In one, a nucleus undergoes decay, explodes the bomb, and wipes us out. But the pigeon holes in that case never contain anything further about life on the Earth ... In the other block [of pigeon holes], *the Earth would be safe, our lives would continue ...*

The image Hoyle paints is of the universe tree as like a living tree, growing all the time and splitting into more and more branches as more choices are opened up. If that picture is correct, anybody who slid back in time could alter the shape of the tree by making changes in the past which caused a new branch, or at least a twig, to start growing from lower down the trunk of the universe tree.

Naturally, science fiction writers thought of this, and they have written many stories using these ideas. One of the most famous is *Lest Darkness Fall* by L. Sprague de Camp. Like *By His Bootstraps*, *Lest Darkness Fall* was first published in 1941. In the book, a time traveller goes back to the time of the Roman Empire, and uses his knowledge about science and technology to make inventions like the printing press, which give a boost to civilization, and makes sure that the Empire doesn't fall.

De Camp uses the analogy that history is like a tree with many branches, down which his time traveller has slid. The history that the traveller creates by introducing technology to Roman times is clearly different to the one he started out from, which is our history. So the author explains that the actions of the traveller have created a new branch of history sprouting from the main trunk, or "time line", of the tree.

It's hard to see what he would mean by the "main time line" of the tree; why should our history be any more special than all the other histories? But even leaving that aside, what quantum physics tells us is that *all* of the alternative histories "always" exist. When the traveller "slides down the trunk", he doesn't start a new branch of history growing out from the universe tree. He arrives at a fork that already exists, and then, because of the combination of choices he makes, he goes up into a different branch from the one he came down. Or, if you like, he moves into a different stack of pigeonholes. But according to quantum physics and the ideas of people like Hugh Everett and Fred Hoyle, all the alternative histories are as real and as important as each other, even though some branches are thicker (that is, more probable histories) than others.

Hold on to the idea of all the possible alternative histories coexisting alongside one another in some kind of "**superspace**", while we bring the science right up to date with the explanation of why light travels in straight lines, and how that makes time travel through wormholes possible without allowing paradoxes. The explanation was discovered by the American physicist Richard Feynman.

Richard Feynman (1918-1988)

Richard Feynman was born on 11 May 1918, in Manhattan, New York. He died on 15 February 1988, in Los Angeles. He was the greatest physicist, and probably the greatest scientist, who lived his life entirely in the twentieth century.

Feynman was encouraged to learn to think like a scientist by his father, Melville, who played scientific games with him and bought a set of the **Encyclopaedia Britannica** *for him to read. His younger sister, Joan, also became a distinguished scientist. He did very well at school, where one of his teachers told him about the Principle of Least Action, even though this wasn't part of the usual course. In 1935, after graduating from high school, Feynman went to the Massachusetts Institute of Technology (MIT) to study physics. He got his degree in 1939, then moved on to Princeton University to work for a PhD. He was a brilliant student, and his professors knew he was something special. As well as being a serious scientist, Richard Feynman was a real party person revelling in having a good time and in entertaining his friends with jokes and stories.*

After the Japanese attack on Pearl Harbor brought the United States in to World War Two in 1941, Feynman was one of the scientists recruited to work on the development of an atomic bomb, which was codenamed the Manhattan Project. He just had time to finish his PhD, in 1942, before moving to Los Alamos, in California, to work on the project. In June 1942, just after getting his PhD and before moving to Los Alamos, he married his childhood sweetheart, Arline Greenbaum, although by then she was ill in hospital with tuberculosis.

At Los Alamos, Richard Feynman made a major contribution to the Manhattan Project, but knew that his wife was dying. The end came in June 1945, not long before the atomic bomb project reached its successful conclusion. Feynman left Los Alamos in November 1945, and took up a post at Cornell University, at Ithaca, New York. It was there that he worked out the theory of light and matter that became known as quantum electrodynamics. At a meeting in Washington shortly afterwards, the physicist Freeman Dyson described QED as "the key to the universe. Quantum electrodynamics works and does everything you wanted it to do. We understand how to calculate everything concerned with electrons and photons."

In 1950, Feynman moved on from Cornell to the California Institute of Technology (Caltech) in Pasadena, where he stayed for the rest of his career. He married Mary Lou Bell in 1952, but the couple divorced in 1956. He had better luck with his third wife, Gweneth, who he married in 1960. This time the marriage lasted, and they had a son, Carl, and an adopted daughter, Michelle.

At Caltech, Feynman continued to make important contributions to science (almost as important as QED), but he also became an inspirational teacher. He gave a series of lectures on physics that were turned into a book, which was published in 1963 and is so good that it is still used by students today. His lectures were like entertainment shows, but packed with information. He also wrote a book for non-scientists about QED, and many of his anecdotes about his life and about science were put together by his friend Ralph Leighton in two best-selling books, Surely You're Joking, Mr. Feynman! and What Do You Care What Other People Think?

When the space shuttle Challenger exploded in 1986, killing the crew, Feynman was recruited to join the *team investigating the disaster. By then he was already ill with cancer and knew that he did not have long to live. But he still played a large part in the investigation, making sure that the team got to the root of the problem that had caused the accident. When he returned home, tired and haggard, he returned to his teaching and other activities. He taught what turned out to be his last class early in 1988, and went in to hospital a few days later. He died on 15 February, with Gweneth, Joan and a cousin, Frances, at his bedside.*

After his cancer was diagnosed, but before the final illness, Feynman told a friend that he wasn't too concerned about dying, because "I feel like I've told enough stories to other people, and enough of me is inside their minds. I've kind of spread me around all over the place. So I'm probably not going to go away completely when I'm dead!"

Richard Feynman's Universe

Richard Feynman was arguably the greatest physicist born in the twentieth century. He lived from 1918 to 1988, and as well as being a great physicist he was also a great storyteller.

Some of his best stories about his life and about science were put together by his friend Ralph Leighton in a book, *Surely You're Joking, Mr Feynman!* Richard Feynman explained how things like atoms, electrons and protons interact with each other and with **electromagnetic radiation**. This is very important because things in the everyday world are made of atoms. Because atoms contain charged particles like protons and electrons, they interact with each other through electricity and magnetism. Electromagnetic forces are what hold atoms and **molecules** together. The theory that describes all this is called **Q**uantum **E**lectro**D**ynamics, or QED. Light is also electromagnetic radiation. So QED is a theory of light and matter and how they interact with one another. It explains everything that is going on in the everyday world except gravity, which is explained by the general theory of relativity. The general theory and QED are the two most successful theories in the whole of science.

QED is amazingly accurate. For example, the theory predicts that something called the magnetic moment of the electron must be a certain number. When experimenters measure the magnetic moment, they get exactly the number that the theory predicts, to an accuracy of ten decimal places, or 0.00000001 per cent. Richard Feynman was fond of pointing out that this accuracy is equivalent to measuring the distance from Los Angeles to New York to the accuracy of the thickness of a human hair. But even QED cannot explain – either with or without the help of the general theory of relativity – what happens at a singularity.

One of the things that made Richard Feynman such an exceptional scientist was that as well as being able to do the hard science, he was very good at communicating his ideas simply and clearly. He had the rare gift of being able to explain his ideas both to other scientists and to people with little or no scientific training. In order to make QED easier to work with and to understand, he invented a new kind of spacetime diagram, similar to the Minkowski diagram. In QED, these are known as **Feynman diagrams**.

In a Feynman diagram, the track through spacetime of a particle like an electron or a proton is represented by a straight line. The track of a photon, a particle of the electromagnetic field, is represented by a wiggly line. Like charges (two negatives, or two positives) repel one another. Because all electrons have negative charge, if two electrons get close to one another they repel each other, "bouncing" away before they actually touch. But in a sense, they *do* touch. QED says that as the electrons get close, they exchange a photon, which travels between them. (It could be more than one photon, of course, but we'll keep it simple for this example.) In a Feynman diagram, this is portrayed by two straight lines (the electrons) moving towards each other, then a wiggly line reaching across between them, and then the two straight lines moving apart.

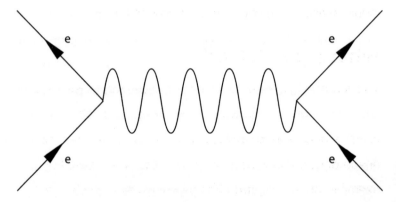

There is also a mathematical way to describe exactly what goes on at the points where the photon interacts with the electrons and they change direction. The diagrams, like the one shown here, give a feel for what is going on without worrying about the equations, and they can be made as complicated as necessary to take account of interactions involving many particles.

But there is one curious feature of the diagrams, which

fascinated Feynman. They have no sense of time. In the diagram shown here, the arrows indicate electrons travelling "up the page", from the past into the future. But as far as QED is concerned, it makes just as much sense to draw the arrows pointing the other way, "down the page", with the particles travelling from the future backwards in time into the past. Feynman diagrams, and QED itself, do not contain any inbuilt sense of direction for the arrow of time.

What's the Matter?

This strange feature of QED is related to another strange scientific phenomenon which often crops up in science fiction stories – **antimatter**. Antimatter is a kind of mirror image of everyday matter, with opposite properties. For example, an anti-electron has a positive electric charge instead of a negative electric charge – so it is often known as a **positron** (it's NOT the same as a proton). It's important to emphasise that antimatter really does exist. Positrons were discovered in the 1930s, and all the other antiparticles predicted by the theory have also been discovered, or made in high-energy collisions in particle accelerators. But antimatter is very rare.

Science fiction writers love the idea, and in many of his

stories Isaac Asimov wrote about robots with "positronic brains". The term is still used by science fiction writers today, but any robot or android that really did have a positronic brain wouldn't last long. The reason why antimatter is rare is that if an antiparticle meets its particle counterpart, the pair of them annihilate one another in a puff of energy. Any positron that exists in the world today will soon meet an electron (any electron will do) and annihilate. An anti-proton will meet up with a proton, and so on. There may once have been more antimatter in the universe, long ago in the Big Bang, but it has all been used up in this way.

The only antimatter found today is made by the opposite process, when there is enough energy around to *make* a pair of particles, such as an electron *and* a positron. For electron-positron pairs, this energy can come from a very energetic photon, called a gamma ray. But any positron produced in this way will soon meet another electron and annihilate to make another gamma ray, so the universe always ends up with the same number of particles. The process of making pairs of antimatter and matter particles can also happen when **cosmic rays** hit the Earth's atmosphere, or in particle accelerators.

Some science fiction writers use the idea of matter-antimatter annihilation to provide the energy for their spaceships. If you had lots of antimatter and you could mix it in tiny drops with ordinary matter, it would produce a blast more powerful than any conventional rocket. But the snag is that to make the antimatter in the first place you would need more energy than you would get out when you let the antimatter annihilate. It isn't a very practical idea.

Richard Feynman discovered a curious thing. As far as the equations of QED are concerned, a positron is exactly the same thing as an electron travelling backwards in time. This means that a Feynman diagram which describes the creation and annihilation of a positron can be read in another way, as a diagram of a single electron travelling in a zig-zag path through time.

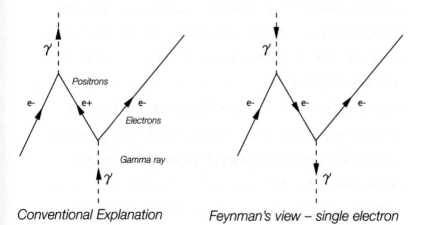

Conventional Explanation   *Feynman's view – single electron*

In the conventional explanation, a **gamma ray** travelling forwards in time turns into an electron and a positron, which go their separate ways. Soon, the positron meets another electron and they annihilate, leaving a gamma ray just like the first one. In Richard Feynman's alternative view, an electron is proceeding steadily forwards in time when it emits a gamma ray and reverses its time direction, travelling back into the past. Then, it interacts with another gamma ray and turns back towards the future. Instead of three particles involved in a kind of dance, there is just one single electron going about its business. Both pictures are entirely equivalent according to QED and all the known laws of physics. Once again, we see that there is nothing in the laws of physics to forbid time travel. But how do the laws of physics make sure that time travel is self-consistent and avoids paradoxes? Feynman has the answer to that, as well.

Light Relief

It all depends on something scientists call "action". The simplest way to understand action is to think of a ball being thrown in a high arc from one person to another. The ball starts out with a lot of kinetic energy, because it is moving at its fastest when it leaves the thrower's hand. As it goes higher it slows down, so the kinetic energy gets less. But at the same time, it has more gravitational energy, because it is farther from the centre of the Earth. This is stored up "potential energy", like the energy in a stretched elastic band. Ignoring friction, the total amount of energy the ball has is always the same. At the top of its arc, it has least kinetic energy but most gravitational potential energy. Then, as it falls down the potential energy is converted into kinetic energy as the ball speeds up until it thumps into the catcher's hand.

The total of the kinetic energy plus the gravitational energy is the same at every point along the flight of the ball, but the *difference* between the two forms of energy is different at every point along the trajectory. If you add up these differences all along the path of the ball, you get the "action" corresponding to that trajectory. The action is a property of the whole trajectory. There is a law of nature called the Principle of Least Action, which says that for a flight that takes a particular time the ball will follow the trajectory with the least action. You can't make the ball take the same time by throwing it higher but faster, or by throwing it lower and slower; there is only one possible trajectory for each flight time.

The Principle of Least Action

In the case of light, the Principle of Least Action is the same as a principle of least time, because light always travels in straight lines. At least, it does in flat space. In curved space, the equivalent of straight lines are called geodesics. They follow the curvature of space. Everything we describe about how light moves in flat space applies to curved space as well.

Light travels slightly faster in air than it does in glass – the absolute speed limit of light applies only in empty space. In either air or glass, light travels in straight lines, which fits the principle of least time because the quickest way to get from A to B is in a straight line. But if the light starts out in air then moves into a block of glass, it has a problem. A single straight line from A to B is not the quickest path.

The quickest path is the one where the light travels as far as possible on a straight line through air rather than glass. If the light spends slightly more time in the air and less in the glass, the extra speed in the air will more than make up for the extra distance it covers. The quickest way from A to B is to take one straight line up to the glass, then another straight line to its destination. There is always just one possible path for the light to take the least time and obey the Principle of Least Action.

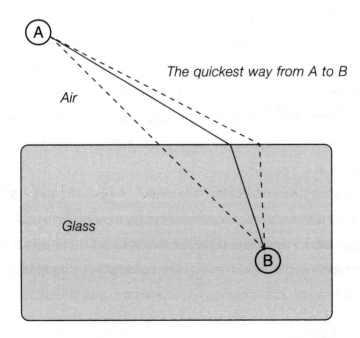

The quickest way from A to B

Air

Glass

The light seems to "know" in advance to travel up to the glass in one straight line, then turn through just the correct angle and carry on to its destination in another straight line. Any other combination of straight lines takes longer. This is another example of the Principle of Least Action at work.

The way the light seems to "know" where it is going and how to get there is similar to the way light and other things seem to "know" about both holes in the experiment with two holes (see page 68), and go through both of them at once. Richard Feynman used the idea of least action to find a way of explaining things like the experiment with two holes. It involves looking at how the effects of different paths through the experiment add up, and it is called "path integrals", because "integral" is another word for "addition".

Historical Sums

Richard Feynman worked out that the *action* for any possible path that a thing like an electron or a photon might take is related to the *probability* of that path.

The probability for the electron going through the experiment with two holes and into a spot on the detector screen is very high, the probability that it will end up on the Moon is very low, and so on. But that only tells you about where the electron starts out and where it ends up. The action is a measurement of the *whole path* from A to B, so it is a number which tells you how the electron actually got from A to B.

Feynman moved on from that to find a way to work out the probabilities of each of the different possible paths from A to B. This is like looking at the whole experiment at once, not just the path through one hole at a time.

This looks like an impossible task, but nature makes it much easier than you might guess. Probabilities behave a bit like waves, so they have amplitudes, corresponding to the height of the wave, like ripples on a pond. These amplitudes can either add together or cancel each other out. Feynman found that the amplitudes cancel each other out in most cases, but around certain paths, they add up. In principle, you have to add up the probability amplitude for every single trajectory, but in practice you only have to worry about the ones that are most likely.

Feynman explained the idea like this. Start out with photons going through the experiment with two holes. The probability of getting a spot of light at a particular place on the detector screen is worked out by adding up, in the right way, the probability amplitudes for paths through each of the two holes. Now make four holes. The calculation gets harder since we have to add up four probability amplitudes, one for each path. With eight holes, we need eight amplitudes, and so on. We can imagine making any number of holes in the screen and adding up all the probabilities in the right way. Or we can take the screen away, so that there is an infinite number of "holes" and an infinite number of paths (and their actions/probabilities) to add up.

Although it is impossible to actually do the sum, Richard Feynman proved that this kind of addition explains how light moves in straight lines. All the other possibilities cancel out! It also explains why the electron in the experiment with two holes doesn't end up on the Moon, or inside some distant star. For every weird path like these, there is a neighbouring path with opposite properties, so the two trajectories cancel each other out. The probabilities only add up for certain paths, which are the ones we see followed by things like balls tossed in the air or electrons going through holes, or light moving from air into a block of glass.

One way of thinking about the experiment with two holes is that when a photon or electron is faced with a choice of which hole to go through, the universe splits in two. In one version of history the photon or electron goes through one hole, in the other version of history it goes through the other.

This solves problems like the puzzle of the fate of Schrödinger's Cat. It is part of the image we have of the universe tree in which all possible histories are real. Feynman said that you have to add up all the probabilities corresponding to different histories in order to work out what is really going on. So this way of picturing what is going on in the quantum world is often called the "sum over histories" idea. "Path integrals" and "sum over histories" are different terms for the same thing – the thing that finally proves that time travel is possible.

Time Pool

Physicists don't like dealing with things like people, or even cats, because they have minds of their own and that makes them unpredictable. The physicists prefer to dream up experiments with inanimate objects that cannot behave in unpredictable ways. So they imagined a version of the granny paradox that involves nothing but pool balls travelling through a suitable time tunnel.

The "experiment" is very simple. Imagine a time tunnel set up with the two mouths quite close together, and a fairly small time difference between them. If a pool ball is rolled into one mouth of the tunnel in just the right way, it will roll out of the other mouth just *before* it enters the tunnel, bump into its younger self, and stop the ball rolling into the hole – see (1). Paradox! This is called a "self-inconsistent solution" to the problem of what happens to pool balls rolled through time tunnels.

(1.) **Ball rolls into tunnel at A, emerges at B and knocks itself off course.**

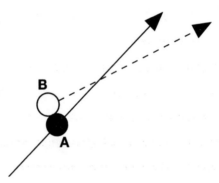

But there are other solutions. Time travel experts like Kip Thorne and the Russian-born researcher Igor Novikov have found that there are always self-*consistent* solutions to these puzzles. For example, a ball might be rolling along near to one entrance to the time tunnel when a ball rolls out of the other entrance and knocks it *into* the tunnel, in such a way that it rolls out of the other mouth and knocks its younger self in to the loop – see (2).

(2.) Ball rolls out of B. Ball rolling near A
   knocks the first ball into A – it emerges at B.

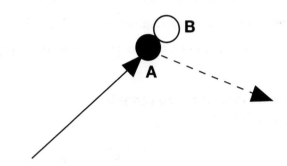

According to Igor Novikov:

If there is a non-self-consistent solution to the
problem and there is also a self-consistent solution,
then nature will choose self-consistency

– and there is *always* a self-consistent solution.

Thorne and Novikov, and their colleagues, have proved
that in every situation where time travel allows for a self-
inconsistent solution, there is always at least one self-
consistent solution. They have proved this mathematically.
Even better, every problem like this that they have dreamed
up so far is proved to have an infinite number of self-
consistent solutions.

   Here's another example. Imagine a ball rolling in a straight
line exactly between the two mouths of the time tunnel.

When it is just between the two mouths, a fast-moving ball comes out of one mouth of the time tunnel, and knocks the first ball straight into the other mouth. But the "second" ball bounces off along the same path the original ball was on. The second ball, is, of course, just the first ball after a trip through time. From far away, if you couldn't see the details, it would still look as if there was just one ball rolling along between the two mouths of the tunnel. You can imagine similar patterns involving two, or three, or as many trips as you like round the loop. From a distance, they all look like a single ball rolling happily on its way.

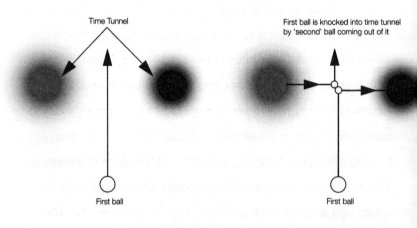

Time Tunnel

First ball

First ball is knocked into time tunnel by 'second' ball coming out of it

First ball

At first, the relativists like Kip Thorne were baffled by this.

There seemed to be a choice of different realities. This isn't what they are used to, at least when dealing with things like pool balls. Then they realised that this is just like the effects that happen in the quantum world, but on a much larger scale. It's like the experiment with two holes, or the Schrödinger's Cat puzzle. When an electron goes through the experiment with two holes, it seems to be perfectly normal until it gets near the two holes, then it interacts with the experiment in a complicated fashion, then it behaves perfectly normally again on the other side.

When a ball goes near a time tunnel it behaves perfectly normally until it gets close to the mouths of the tunnel. When it arrives there it interacts with the tunnel in complicated ways, then it simply rolls on perfectly normally again on the other side. It's like quantum physics with pool balls instead of electrons. Once they realised that, the physicists knew just how to deal with these complications, using Feynman's sum over histories technique.

The sum over histories, or path integral, technique works perfectly when it is applied to time-travelling pool balls. It gives you a set of probabilities telling you where and when the ball will be most (or least) likely to emerge on the other side, clear of the region in which time travel is going on. This is just like the way quantum physics tells you where on the detector screen the electrons are likely to end up in the experiment with two holes.

It doesn't tell you *how* the ball gets through the time-travel region, any more than quantum physics tells you *how* an electron gets through the experiment with two holes. In a sense, the ball "chooses" one path in each experiment, and the rules predict the probability of each path. Or, the universe tree forks into thicker and thinner branches in line with the probabilities, always in a self-consistent way.

But there is one more strange prediction of the sum over histories solution to the puzzles of time travel. It is also a sum over *futures*, because the ball travels in time. If there is a time tunnel available there are more paths that the ball could follow than if there is no time tunnel. According to Thorne's calculations this means that even before the ball gets to the tunnel, the probabilities will be changed and its behaviour will be slightly different. The effects would be extremely tiny, but Kip Thorne says that in principle they could be measured. Measuring the effects would certainly be easier than building a time machine.

This means that in years to come, if physicists can devise the right experiments, they will be able to make measurements on things like pool balls that will tell them if a time machine is going to be invented – even if nobody has any idea how to make a practical time machine. They will know something about the future, without actually travelling in time.

Waiting for a Time Machine

How long might it be before an actual time machine is built? In his book *Black Holes and Time Warps*, Kip Thorne says that time machines "are probably much farther beyond the human race's present technological capabilities than space travel was beyond the capabilities of cavemen."

Does he mean that, even if time travel is allowed by the laws of physics, actually building a time machine is impossibly hard? Not necessarily. The Palaeolithic, the time of cavemen, ended less than 15,000 years ago, and the Sun and the Earth are likely to be around for billions of years yet to come. That gives mankind thousands of times longer than the time since cavemen were around in which to build a time machine or two. The science fiction writer Arthur C. Clarke summed it up:

When a distinguished but elderly scientist states that something is possible, he is almost certainly right. When he states that something is impossible, he is very probably wrong.

Glossary

Antimatter A kind of mirror image version of the kind of matter we are made of, with reversed properties. For example, an anti-electron (also known as a positron) has positive electric charge instead of negative electric charge.

Atom The smallest component of everyday matter that takes part in chemical reactions. All elements, such as oxygen or iron, are made of particular kinds of atoms. Each atom is made up of a tiny central *nucleus* surrounded by a cloud of *electrons*.

Binary system A pair of stars, or a star and a *black hole*, orbiting around one another.

Black hole A region of *spacetime* bent round on itself by gravity so that nothing, not even light, can escape.

Casimir Effect A way of making negative energy by putting two metal plates close together in a vacuum.

CERN The European particle accelerator laboratory near Geneva, where beams of particles are collided head-on in "atom smashing" experiments. Among many other achievements, these experiments have proved that *time dilation* and the *twin effect* are real.

Chandrasekhar limit The maximum mass for a *white dwarf*, equivalent to 1.4 times the mass of our Sun.

Classical physics The rules and equations that apply to things much bigger than *atoms* (but not in the region of time machines!).

Closed timelike line (CTL) A path through spacetime that ends up back where it started in both space *and* time.

Cosmic rays Energetic particles from space that hit the Earth's atmosphere.

Einstein-Rosen bridge Another name for a *wormhole*.

Electromagnetic radiation Any form of radiation, including light, radio waves and X-rays, that is made up of electricity and magnetism, described by *Maxwell's equations*.

Electron A tiny particle with negative electric charge. Electrons can also behave as waves. See *atom*.

Exotic material or matter Matter which contains negative energy, and produces antigravity. Exotic matter pushes ordinary matter away from itself, instead of attracting it.

Extension The equivalent of length in four dimensions, involving time as well as the three dimensions of space.

Feynman diagram A special kind of *spacetime diagram* which portrays the way particles like *electrons* and *protons* interact with each other by exchanging *photons*.

Gamma rays Very energetic *electromagnetic radiation*, more powerful than X-rays.

General theory of relativity The laws that describe what happens to things moving in any kind of curved path, or straight lines, at any speed or acceleration. Because acceleration and *gravity* are equivalent, the same laws explain how *gravity* works, and how *spacetime* can be distorted to make *black holes* and *wormholes*.

Geodesics The equivalent in curved space of straight lines in flat space. Light always follows geodesics.

Gravitational energy The energy something has because of its position near matter. It takes an effort to lift something up off the ground, because you are moving it farther away from the centre of the Earth. That effort becomes stored-up gravitational energy. When you let go of the object it falls down and the extra gravitational energy is turned into *kinetic energy*.

Gravity The force that makes lumps of matter attract one another. For example, the Earth pulls on your body, but your body also pulls on the Earth. Albert Einstein explained how gravity works using the *general theory of relativity*.

Interference pattern The pattern made when two sets of waves overlap. This could be, for example, ripples on a pond, or light spreading out from two holes in a piece of cardboard.

Kinetic energy The energy something has because it is moving.

Length contraction The way the length of a moving object shrinks along the direction of its motion.

Light year The distance travelled by light in one year, 9.46 million million km. A light year is a measure of distance, not of time.

Many Worlds Hypothesis The idea that there are many different versions of reality, sometimes called parallel universes, somehow lying "next door" to each other like the pages in a book.

Maxwell's equations A set of equations that describe the way electricity and magnetism behave. In particular, the equations tell us what the speed of light is, because light is a form of *electromagnetic radiation*.

Minkowski diagram A way of representing the movement of things through *spacetime* on a kind of graph, or map.

Molecule A group of *atoms* held together in a stable unit by electromagnetic forces.

Momentum The mass of an object multiplied by its velocity.

Neutron A neutral particle found in the *nucleus* of an *atom*.

Neutron star A kind of dead star. Each cubic centimetre of a neutron star would have a mass of a hundred million tonnes. The maximum possible mass for a neutron star is about three times the mass of our Sun.

Nucleus The central part of an *atom*, made up of *protons* and *neutrons*.

Parallel universe See *Many Worlds Hypothesis*.

Photon A particle of light, or of any electromagnetic field or wave.

Planck's constant A very small number, usually written as *h*, that relates the wavelength of a quantum object, such as an electron, to its momentum.

Planck length The smallest possible size for anything, the *quantum* of size. In centimetres, roughly a decimal point followed by 32 zeroes and a 1.

Planck scale General term for anything roughly the size of the *Planck length*.

Positron The *antimatter* counterpart to the *electron*.

Proton A positively charged particle found in the *nucleus* of an *atom*.

Pulsar A spinning *neutron star* that emits pulses of radio noise, like a radio lighthouse in space.

Quantum The smallest amount of anything that can exist. A *photon*, for example, is a quantum of light.

Quantum electrodynamics (QED) The theory of light

and matter that explains how *atoms* and *molecules* work.

Quantum leap The smallest change it is possible to make.

Quantum physics The laws and equations that describe the way small things like *electron*s and *atoms* behave.

Schrödinger's Cat A mythical cat that, according to one version of *quantum physics*, can be dead and alive at the same time.

Schwarzschild radius The radius of a *black hole*.

Singularity A point with zero volume, or a line with zero width.

Spacetime The unification of the three dimensions of space and the fourth dimension of time, described by the *general theory of relativity*.

Spacetime diagram See *Minkowski diagram*, *Feynman diagram*.

Special theory of relativity The laws that describe what happens to things moving in straight lines at constant speeds. This sounds boring, but it turns out that at high speeds time runs slow and moving objects shrink. See also *general theory of relativity*.

Superspace Something beyond our dimensions of *spacetime* in which our space is embedded. If a book is like superspace, one page of the book would be our space.

Time dilation The way time stretches out for a moving object, so that moving clocks run slow.

Twin effect If one of two identical twins goes on a long journey at nearly the speed of light, when he or she gets home the travelling twin will be younger than the twin who stayed at home, because of *time dilation*.

Velocity A measure of both the speed an object is moving at, and the direction it is moving in.

White dwarf A kind of dead star. The Sun will end its life as a white dwarf. One cubic centimetre of white dwarf matter would have a mass of about 1 tonne

Wormhole A tunnel through *spacetime* joining two *black holes*.

Further Reading

Books marked * are mostly more technical, but still contain some easier sections about time travel.

Books marked + are fiction, but explore some of the scientific ideas we describe in our book.

Adrian Berry, *The Iron Sun*, Cape, London, 1977.

+Ray Bradbury, "A Sound of Thunder", in *The Stories of Ray Bradbury*, Knopf, New York, 1980.

+L. Sprague de Camp, *Lest Darkness Fall*, Holt, New York, 1941.

Lewis Carroll Epstein, *Relativity Visualized*, Insight Press, San Francisco, revised edition, 1987.

*Paul Davies, *About Time*, Viking, London, 1995.

+Philip K. Dick. *The Man in the High Castle*, Gollancz, London, 1975.

Richard Feynman & Ralph Leighton, *Surely You're Joking, Mr Feynman!*, Norton, New York, 1985.

George Gamow, *Mr Tompkins in Paperback*, Cambridge UP, 1993.

+David Gerrold, *The Man Who Folded Himself*, BenBella Books, New York, 2003.

George Greenstein, *Frozen Star*, Freundlich, New York, 1984.

John Gribbin, *Quantum Physics: A beginner's guide*, Dorling Kindersley, London, 2002.

+John Gribbin, *TimeSwitch*, PS Publishing, London, 2009.

John & Mary Gribbin, *Einstein in 90 minutes*, Constable, London, 1997.

John & Mary Gribbin, *Time and Space*, Dorling Kindersley, London, 1994.

Stephen Hawking, *Black Holes and Baby Universes*, Bantam, London, second edition, 1994.

+Robert Heinlein, "By His Bootstraps", in *The Astounding-Analog Reader Book One*, edited by Harry Harrison and Brian Aldiss, Sphere, London, 1973.

Nick Herbert, *Quantum Reality*, Rider, London, 1985.

+Fred Hoyle, *October the First is Too Late*, Heinemann, London, 1966.

*Michio Kaku, *Hyperspace*, OUP, New York, 1994.

+Michael Moorcock, *Behold the Man*, Mayflower, London, 1970.

+Ward Moore, *Bring the Jubilee*, Equinox/Avon, New York, 1976.

+Larry Niven, *A World out of Time*, Macdonald & Jane's, London, 1977.

Time Travel for Beginners

+Larry Niven, *Convergent Series*, Ballantyne, New York, 1979.

Barry Parker, *Einstein's Dream*, Plenum, New York, 1986.

+Carl Sagan, *Contact*, Simon & Schuster, New York, 1985.

+Clifford Simak, *Time and Again*, Simon & Schuster, New York, 1951.

Russell Stannard, *Black Holes and Uncle Albert*, Faber & Faber, London, 2005.

John Taylor, *Black Holes*, Souvenir, London, 1973.

+H. G. Wells, *The Time Machine*, Penguin Classics, London, 2005 (originally published in 1895).

*Kip Thorne, *Black Holes and Time Warps*, Picador, London, 1994.

Index